MISSIONS AND SERVICE PROJECTS

Jim Burns and Mike Devries

GENERAL
EDITOR

COMPILER

Gospel Light

Gospel Light is an evangelical Christian publisher dedicated to serving the local church. We believe God's vision for Gospel Light is to provide church leaders with biblical, user-friendly materials that will help them evangelize, disciple and minister to children, youth and families.

We hope this Gospel Light resource will help you discover biblical truth for your own life and help you minister to youth. God bless you in your work.

For a free catalog of resources from Gospel Light please contact your Christian supplier or contact us at 1-800-4-GOSPEL, *or at* www.gospellight.com.

PUBLISHING STAFF
William T. Greig, Publisher
Dr. Elmer L. Towns, Senior Consulting Publisher
Dr. Gary S. Greig, Senior Consulting Editor
Jill Honodel, Editor
Pam Weston, Assistant Editor
Patti Virtue, Editorial Assistant
Kyle Duncan, Associate Publisher
Bayard Taylor, M.Div., Senior Editor, Theological and Biblical Issues
Barbara LeVan Fisher, Cover Designer
Debi Thayer, Designer

ISBN 0-8307-1879-6
© 1999 by Jim Burns
All rights reserved.
Printed in U.S.A.

HOW TO MAKE CLEAN COPIES FROM THIS BOOK

Contents

Contents

Dedication

To Jeff and Jill Fears, missionaries, fellow workers in Christ, and most of all, my dear friends: I love you both so very much. Our friendship means the world to me. May God use you mightily in the lives of the people of Poland.

Thanks and Thanks Again!

To the hundreds of students who have traveled with us on mission trips and retreats: The memories we have, we'll share for a lifetime.

To my wife, Jamie, and my children, Joshua and Megan: I thank God every day for giving me the greatest family I could ever ask for. I love you. Thanks for "loaning" Daddy for a little while during the writing and editing of this book.

To Jill Fears: Thanks for all the late hours and phone calls it took to type this manuscript. Thanks for all your work in making this project a reality.

Contributors

Craig Deane
Craig has been in youth ministry for 16 years and is currently Pastor of Family Ministries at La Habra Hills Presbyterian Church. He has also been involved in ministry in Poland, the Czech Republic, Venezuela, the Dominican Republic, Colombia, Brazil and Australia. Craig lives with his wife Kathleen and their dog and cat in La Habra, California.

Mike DeVries
Mike serves as Pastor of High School Ministries at the Yorba Linda Friends Church in Orange County, California. A former youth trainer, Mike and his family live in Southern California.

Chriss Peterson
Chriss has been a youth pastor for 18 years, serving the past 12 of those years as Director of Youth Ministries at St. Ansgar's Lutheran Church in Salinas, California. He and his wife Elizabeth have two young daughters, Anna and Rachel.

Mark A. Simone
Mark has been ministering to young people in Ohio for over 18 years. Mark also compiled *Case Studies, Talk Sheets and Discussion Starters*, volume 2 in the *Fresh Ideas* series. He is author of *Ministering to Kids Who Don't Fit* and, with his wife Kathy, is coauthor of the book *Teaching Today's Youth*. Mark and Kathy have two sons and two daughters.

Contributors' Submissions

Craig Deane
Mission and Service Projects

Mike DeVries
The Short-Term Missions Handbook

Mark A. Simone
Work Camps

Chriss Peterson
Missions and Service Resources
The Acts 1:8 Model for Missions
Bible References for Studies on Missions and Service
Bibliographies

Introduction

It has often been said that more and better Christian education takes place in a couple of weekend work camps or one mission service project than in an entire year of Sunday School. The reason you probably picked up this excellent resource is because you know how important mission experiences can be to the spiritual growth of your students. Mike DeVries has brought together a plethora of outstanding and practical ideas for mission, work camp and service projects. As I read over every sentence, I continued to get excited that you have available to you very practical ideas from some of America's finest youth workers on subjects you will definitely be able to use. Better yet, the experiences in this book have already been used with students, and they worked!

If you are new to youth work, then you will appreciate the practical how-tos from *A* to *Z*. If you are a veteran, then I know you will enjoy being able to find a new handle on the important information in this book. Thank you, my fellow youth worker, for your continued influence in the lives of students. Who knows—one of these experiences may be just the thing that turns a student's life toward God and makes an eternal difference. Thanks for your commitment to kids and families.

Jim Burns, Ph.D.
President, National Institute
of Youth Ministry

Missions and Service Projects

Participating in a mission project is one of the most life-transforming experiences a student can have. Over the past nine years in ministry at our church, we've taken hundreds of students to serve cross-culturally, to share the love of Christ, and to see lives transformed by the love of Jesus. Dramatic things happen in the lives of students when they are placed in a situation where they have to completely and trustingly put themselves in God's hands. They will see God at work. They will experience His dramatic answers to prayer. Their lives will be changed!

At the end of every school year we have a senior banquet. It's a time for our graduating seniors to celebrate what God has done in their lives and a chance for us to recognize them for an evening. At every banquet we give our seniors an opportunity to share what has impacted them the most in being a part of the high school ministry. Every year mission trips are one of the most frequently talked about experiences that have impacted their lives. Learning to serve God and others changes lives—something students desperately need in this "me-first" world.

Whether you've never experienced a mission trip before or you're a seasoned veteran of dirt floors, airports, long van rides, construction projects, cross-cultural Vacation Bible Schools, three-hour church services in a totally mysterious foreign language, we pray that the following ideas will challenge you, sharpen you and impact your students as you place them in the hands of God on the mission field.

We have included in this section ideas for both service and mission projects. The best way to develop a heart for missions and service is to begin with smaller service projects in and around your community, then graduate to weekend work camps and move on to short-term mission trips. This section will provide invaluable ideas and information for everything from collecting food for a homeless shelter to building houses in Mexico.

The Basics of Missions and Service

Motivating Young People to Serve

Several years ago I took twenty high school students on a short-term mission trip to the jungles of Venezuela in South America. All of us gave up our summer to build a mission home, lead Bible studies and work with Indian children. It was a seven-week adventure complete with love, service, learning, laughter and spiritual growth. Today sixteen of those twenty students are involved in some type of Christian service. I believe they are involved in Christian service today because of the mission exposure they received while they were still young and impressionable.

Since that trip to South America, I've taken hundreds of young people on mission trips. And I've watched the majority of these young people experience a profound life change because of what God does in them (and me) through serving others. One of our most important tasks as youth workers is to get young people involved in missions and service.

Begin with the easier two-hour service projects, building interest and commitment as you gradually provide more and more challenging projects and trips.

Model Missions and Service

The apostle Paul said "Follow my example, as I follow the example of Christ" (1 Corinthians 11:1). Young people are watching and following our examples. If we want our students to become excited about missions and service, our life example should point them toward missions and service. Volunteer in the community, become a member of organizations such as Rotary, and work with food banks or at residential care homes. Be a living example of serving with the love of Christ and your students will "catch the fire."

Help Young People Develop a Servant's Heart

We live in an age of selfishness. Many of the young people we work with are growing up in an environment that promotes self-indulgence. As our young people mature in their Christian faith, we must help them face the fact that God's ways are different than the world's. The world tells them to look out for Number One. The call of Christ is the call to serve others. After all, it was Christ who announced that His purpose for coming to this world was to serve others. "For even the Son of Man did not come to be served,

but to serve, and to give his life as a ransom for many" (Mark 10:45). We have a responsibility to help students look past themselves and focus their attention on God and other people. We must help them develop a compassionate servant's heart for their friends, relatives, neighbors and strangers.

Create an Awareness of Missions and Service

Many students have a distorted view of missions and service. For them it means selling all their possessions, wearing ugly, cast-off clothes and flying to the jungles of Africa to proclaim the Word of God to a village of naked people. It is our obligation to clear up misconceptions and help students become aware of the need for missions and service wherever they are. The way to do this is by teaching regularly on the topics of missions and service. Bring in exciting and relevant guest speakers that you have already screened. Expose your students to one of the many inspirational films on missions today. Teach on the life of one of the greatest missionaries ever, the apostle Paul. Take your students to the inner city and show them firsthand how people live in poverty. These are all simple ways to heighten students' awareness of missions and service. (Refer to the "Mission and Service Resources" on pages 127-146.)

Start Small with the Young People Who Are Motivated

When it comes time to plan your first mission and/or service project, don't bite off more than you can chew. Most of the time it is best to start small. Remember that many students are nervous about something that is new and different. A wise first project can include a brief trip to a rest home or a visit to a local soup kitchen. Don't worry about large numbers. Take the students who are interested in getting involved in missions and service. Once the young people have experienced missions firsthand, they will spread the joy and excitement to the rest of the group and spark the interest of their peers.

Selecting a Project

Know What You Want to Do

Before you can decide where you want to go, you must decide what you want to do. In order to plan well, you must ask the right questions. Here are a few basic questions to ask yourself when planning a mission project:

- What are your goals for the trip?
- Are you interested in building your youth group's leadership base?
- Do you want to work only with those students who are interested in missions and service?
- Is it your desire to involve your students evangelistically? If so, begin with a project that involves telling Bible stories to children or door-to-door evangelism.
- Or do you prefer to concentrate on physical needs? Then choose a soup kitchen or home-building project.
- Is your objective to expose your students to a cross-cultural experience or to involve them in some type of entry-level service project?
- How far can you realistically travel?
- How long of a project do you want to organize? One day? A long weekend? A week? Or all summer?
- How much money do you want to spend on the trip? How much money can you realistically expect students to pay/earn?

Once you have defined the objectives of your project, you are ready to choose a project type and site.

Looking for Project Opportunities

Now that you have decided what you want to do, begin the search for a project. The next section includes dozens of ideas that will help you get started. You may also find a potential project by contacting missionaries from your own church or denomination. Project ideas begin on page 23.

   If your group has never done a service or mission project, choose a project that takes the youth group out of its comfort zone but not so far out that they won't want to participate in the next project. Discuss the options with the students and decide together what they can realistically accomplish.

Visit the Project Site

If at all possible, personally visit the project site yourself before the actual trip. This can be time-consuming and at times expensive, but it is extremely important. The ministry site explained by phone or letter can be drastically different from what you discover when you see it firsthand.

In 1989 I was planning on taking a small service team to an elderly woman's home about an hour's drive from our church. I made arrangements with her over the phone to clear the patio of overgrown ivy and paint the patio cover. The project would take one day to complete and everything sounded great, but when I visited the site two weeks before the trip, I discovered an impossible situation. The ivy had entangled itself so tightly onto the patio cover that the two had become fused. It would have been futile to try to remove the ivy without replacing the patio cover. The project was too advanced for the skills of our small ministry team. I gently explained the situation to the homeowner and changed my plans to an alternate home project that we could realistically handle.

Receive Final Approval

The first person you will want to consult is your senior pastor or immediate supervisor. Involving the pastor or your supervisor demonstrates your respect for his or her authority and wisdom. With your supervisor on your side it is much easier to gain final approval from the church's governing body.

Once you have informed the pastor or your immediate supervisor, arrange an appointment with the mission committee if your church has one. Often they can help with financing the project and offer advice for the final planning of the project.

Finally, inform and seek approval from the other governing boards and committees as required by your church (i.e., Christian education committee and the elder board). Informing the proper church leadership will help them have more confidence in your leadership.

Publicity

Once you have selected a ministry project, it is important to spread the news of the project to the youth group, the parents and the church body.

Flyers and Brochures

Besides verbally announcing the project, put together a flyer or brochure explaining the project. You may not be an expert in graphics and design, but there is a good chance that somebody in your congregation can help you put together an informative and attractive flyer or brochure.

For longer projects I suggest requiring an application form to be completed by the students and their parents or guardians. I also recommend including at least two personal reference forms to be completed by a peer and an adult (teacher, coach, employer, etc.) other than the parents.

Parental Awareness Is Key

It is very important that you communicate clearly and consistently to the parents of the young people about the project. For small projects we suggest you inform the parents by letter and phone calls. The letter should apprise the parents of all the pertinent information, including the date, time, location, cost, purpose of the trip and a site phone number to contact in case of emergencies. A follow-up phone call will help the parents feel more comfortable about the project as well as open the door for future relationship-building opportunities.

For longer mission and service projects we always recommend an introductory parents' information meeting in addition to the letter and phone call.

Involve the Entire Church

Publicize the mission or service project to your congregation at large. Use your church's best forms of mass communication (bulletin, pulpit and/or newsletter announcement) to inform the church about the upcoming youth mission project. Encourage the congregation to pray for the students on a regular basis.

For longer projects make up prayer cards for each participant and distribute them to members during the church's regular worship service. Have one or two students share the progress with the congregation in a short two- to three-minute testimonial. This will build the congregation's awareness of the trip, making prayer support and the necessary fund-raising more acceptable.

Selecting and Training the Team

Selection of Adult Leaders

Mission and service projects require more adult participation than most youth activities. The more adults you have involved with the project—one adult to every five students is a good ratio—the smoother your project will run. Therefore, it is important to start your team-building process by selecting the right adult leaders for the project. Carefully select an adult staff that will help train, facilitate, nurture and encourage the students on the project team. Try to get firm commitments from leaders as early as possible. Remember that your adult staff will strongly influence the attitude and direction of your team. Choose adults who are Christ-centered, people- and youth-oriented, and team players.

Selection of Student Participants

If the majority of your students have never served on a project, it is better to sensitize them to the needs of the world through a small trip to a convalescent hospital or a simple yard-cleaning project. As your students gain mission and service experience, challenge them to more advanced projects such as an inner city Vacation Bible School program or a short-term mission project at a Native American reservation or across the border in Mexico. It is important that we believe in our students and challenge them to grow in their faith by providing quality mission and service opportunities. Know each student before the trip; contract with students concerning your expectations for the trip and their behavior.

Spiritual Preparation

You should never overlook students' spiritual development as an important dimension of missions and service. Paul told his young disciple Timothy to "train yourself to be godly" (1 Timothy 4:7). The goal of youth ministry is to help students spiritually discipline themselves, as individuals and as team members.

Encourage your students to study the Bible and pray on a regular basis. More specifically, choose a chapter or book of the Bible to focus on before and during the trip. Set aside certain devotional readings each day for students to focus on (see pp. 144-145 for a list of Bible study ideas). Also, have the team pray *together* on a regular basis, relinquishing every part of the service opportunity to God.

Do everything you can to build group unity with the team before the project begins. A unified group will more effectively minister to other people. Stimulate unity in your group by conducting Bible studies that focus on unity.

For longer projects, plan several training meetings. You may also want to program a weekend retreat that will concentrate on building a spiritual foundation and community

within your group. Have the students sign a "team covenant" at the retreat. The covenant is a contract between the group members, describing the team members' commitments to God and each other.

Encourage students to keep a prayer journal through every step of the preparations and the project/trip. Remember, this opportunity will be one of the most significant spiritual events in the students' lives. Some examples of suggestions for their journal assignments might be:

- Reflect on the meaning of the verses of the Bible you are reading for the trip;
- Write down specific prayers or prayer requests for the team/team members;
- Write down specific prayers or prayer requests for people met during the trip.

Task Preparation

It is important to properly prepare your students for the necessary tasks involved in your project. Paul Borthwick, in his book, *Youth and Missions*, explains, "The success of a service project, mission team, or even a workday is often determined before the van leaves the church parking lot or the plane takes off. The key is in the preparation of both leaders and students."[1]

If your students are involved in a construction project, have a construction worker in your congregation conduct a workshop on the basics of construction. If your team will be running a Vacation Bible School program, make sure they practice their stories, skits, crafts and games before they get to the project site. The more prepared your students are, the more impact they will make on the people they are ministering to.

Cross-Cultural Preparation

If you choose a project that involves cross-cultural exposure, it is important to adequately prepare your students and leaders to be culturally sensitive. If you are working with an established mission organization, they will most likely have some basic cultural information available to present to students during the team training meetings. When teaching on cultural sensitivity try to keep two things in mind: (1) a culture can be different from our culture without either culture being judged "right" or "wrong"; (2) exposure to a different culture helps us learn more about our own culture and be more sensitive to the differences within our own culture.

Note:
1. Paul Borthwick, *Youth and Missions* (Wheaton, Ill.: Victor Books, 1988), p. 95.

Financing the Project

Adequate financing for your project is important to a successful experience. Fund-raising has become a necessary task in youth ministry. Like it or not, it is part of the territory. If you find it necessary to conduct a fund-raiser in order to finance your project, here are a few helpful suggestions:

Plan a Budget

Develop a simple "Project Budget Worksheet" that lists all possible expenses. A sample budget worksheet can be found beginning on page 80 in the Short-Term Missions Handbook section. Check with your church treasurer or finance department to see if they already have a form or worksheet available. Your worksheet should include the following categories:

- Transportation (tolls, gasoline, air travel, land travel, etc.)
- Food
- Housing
- Equipment (tools, teaching materials, instruments, costumes, etc.)
- Supplies (paint, cement, etc.)

After you've carefully estimated the total cost of your project, record your results in a format that can be understood by your church.

Seek Adequate Funding

You will most likely fund your trip in one or any combination of the following three ways: through the church's youth or mission budget, the student participants themselves (or their parents) and/or fund-raising projects. For more expensive projects it is advisable to seek funding from all three sources. It is important to require your students to work for some amount of their project funding. This teaches young people important lessons on responsibility and trust in God.

We also advise that you make allowances to pay for the adult leaders' expenses. It is expecting too much to require leaders to give up time from their busy schedules and then ask them to pay for their participation in the project as well.

If you are planning on requesting funding from the mission committee of your church, put together a project proposal (see pp. 37-38) that includes the purpose of the project, goals and objectives of the project, the expected number of adult and student participants, the project site and a project budget worksheet.

Fund-raising can be done by the group and/or the individuals themselves. Some basic fund-raising projects include support letter writing, pancake breakfast, walk-a-thon,

garage sale, flower/plant sales, youth sponsors, auction and a car wash. Be creative with your fund-raisers. Make sure you have the student and adult participants take leadership of the chosen fund-raising projects. If people in your church sponsor individual participants in the project, make sure the students update them before, during and after the trip. Have the participants write thank-you notes to each sponsor. This teaches the participants responsibility and lets the sponsors know that their money was spent on a worthwhile project.

Develop a Record-Keeping System

Even small projects require a number of financial transactions. Therefore it is pertinent that you develop a system that allows you to record all financial transactions. If bookkeeping is not your strength, recruit a skilled student, adult participant or parent to handle this important task for you. Your church's financial leaders will thank you! A simple way to do record keeping is as follows:

Income	Expenditures
Earnings from each fundraiser	Preparations for project
Budgeted funds for projects	Food
Donations from church organizations	Transportation
Student payments	Tools/Supplies
	Miscellaneous/Emergencies

During the Project

Attitude Is Everything!

Your attitude and the attitude of the other adult leaders will set the tone for the project. The following are five guidelines that serve to set the proper tone of mission and service opportunities:

- **Be flexible.** Things can and often do go wrong on mission and service trips. Be flexible with your expectations and let God teach you *His* expectations.
- **Work hard, then play hard.** We go on service projects to work, but young people need to have fun. Set goals at the beginning of each project and encourage students to accomplish those goals. Afterward, reward your students with a big dose of fun.
- **Be positive.** A negative attitude spreads throughout the team like a wildfire in dry grass. As adult leaders, try to keep the mood upbeat and positive. Take care of conflicts and problems as soon as possible to avoid a build up of resentments.

- **Be enthusiastic.** Show interest in the project and the people you meet on-site. Don't sit on the sidelines watching students and adults do all the work. Be the first and last person involved in the project.
- **Be godly.** It is possible to go out on a short project and leave God at home. Remember the purpose of the trip is to allow others and ourselves to experience God. Start and complete each project with prayer and a devotional. Pray continuously throughout the day. Interject Scripture at appropriate times during the project.

Debrief Each Day's Experience

The students are processing a lot of new information throughout the mission experience. Therefore, it is important to give them an opportunity to talk about their feelings after the project is completed. If your project lasts more than one day, give young people and leaders a chance to share their experiences with each other at the end of each day.

At times you will find it necessary to gently admonish some students. It is inevitable that students will get on each other's nerves or get a little carried away with horseplay. Our philosophy is to be consistent with reproach and nip problems in the bud. Keep any confrontation as positive as possible. Don't neglect admonishment as an important part of the debriefing process. The debriefing process helps students apply faith lessons and develop self-control in their everyday lives.

Project Etiquette

Students have an incredible amount of energy and enthusiasm. Sometimes their excitement causes them to forget about who they are serving—the Lord and the Lord's people. Therefore it is important to remind students to respect all people (including other team members) and property while serving the Lord. Help team members develop and maintain attitudes that exemplify kindness and consideration. Remind them of their witness—that everything they do will influence people, either positively or negatively, toward God.

Mission Trip Hints

You may want to plan an extra day to do some sight-seeing or to enjoy the special attractions of the area as a reward for a week of hard work.

Plan a devotional and debriefing time each evening to process the day's events and to learn from the experience.

From the moment the trip is announced, emphasize the importance of the mission. This is not a vacation. It can be a great time of fun and memory making, but remember that the mission comes first.

After the Project Is Over

Evaluations

As the trip comes to an end, include a time for the students and leaders to evaluate the project. Put together an evaluation form (see pp. 91-94) that will give you feedback on the positives and negatives of the project. Don't be afraid to ask students and adult leaders tough questions. For example: How did the project meet your original goals? What did they learn about missions and service? How were they challenged spiritually? Did you have adequate leadership for the project? What elements of the project worked well? What would you do differently next time?

Once you have evaluated the project, record the results and make the proper adjustments on future projects. I have learned some of youth ministry's most valuable lessons through mission and service projects.

Follow-Up with the Team

The project is not done when the students go back home with their families. Many students make significant decisions about their faith during a mission or service project. It is important to follow up with each student regarding his or her experience. If the trip lasts a week or more, it is not uncommon for students to experience loneliness or depression a week or two after the trip. Schedule personal appointments with each student within the first week or two after the project in order to give them an opportunity to talk about their feelings and decisions. Proper follow-up is crucial in maintaining spiritual growth and fervor in your students. Keep them accountable for any decisions made.

Plan a team reunion a week or two after the trip. Be sure to take slides/videos during your project and have the team members bring their photos or slides to the reunion. Give opportunities for students to share things they learned, decisions they made or favorite anecdotes. Plan a dinner/party after the trip to thank the church family for their support and encouragement.

Follow-Up with the Congregation

After returning from a project, it is important to share your experiences with the congregation. If possible, arrange a time in your worship service to allow students to share about the project with the congregation. Insert an information article about the project in the church bulletin/newsletter. Be sure to include students' and adult leaders' personal comments and stories.

If your project involved prayer partners, have students send their partners follow-up letters. Include a picture of the student at the project site. Proper follow-up with the congregation will help them more readily approve and support the youth program in general, and future mission and service opportunities in particular.

Missions and Service Project Ideas

Missions to the Elderly

Adopt a Grandparent

There are many elderly people who are living a long distance from their relatives and desire companionship and attention. After developing a list of elderly people in your congregation or visiting a local convalescent home, introduce the concept of "adopting" one or more of these elderly people as a "grandparent." Adoption can include regular visitation, remembering special dates and holidays, running errands, preparing an occasional meal and simply being there as a friend for a designated period of time.

Adopt a Home

Churches often have elderly or disabled members who are unable to adequately care for their homes and yards. Invite your group to "adopt" the home of a needy person in your congregation or community. Adoption can include general yard care, sweeping the sidewalks and patios, general interior cleaning, window washing, carpet cleaning, floor waxing, interior and/or exterior painting, changing furnace filters, moving furniture, seasonal decorating (Christmas-tree trimming), changing burned-out light bulbs, and installation or inspection of battery-operated smoke detectors.

Senior Appreciation Banquet

This is a great way to honor the elderly people in your church. Have the youth group members plan a banquet and program and invite the senior citizens of your church to be their guests. In order to use as many of the students as possible, the group may be divided into task groups with each group performing a necessary function. The task groups should include: publicity and invitations, decorations, setup, cleanup, food preparation, program/entertainment and transportation.

The dinner could either be potluck, catered or prepared by the students/parents. The program should be short and entertaining. You may need to provide transportation for some of your guests who aren't able to drive anymore. With some hard work and enthusiasm, the banquet can become a yearly tradition at your church.

Missions to Children

Church Nursery Makeover

The nursery is one of the first things young families see when they visit a church. If your church nursery needs a makeover or just a thorough cleaning, dedicate a workday to renovating or cleaning the nursery. A makeover can include cleaning the carpet or floor, scrubbing and/or painting the woodwork and walls, cleaning the windows, cleaning and disinfecting the toys, painting the furniture, cleaning, repairing and replacing the bedding. Experienced seamstresses could make new cushions and curtains that compliment the color scheme of the room. The children and their parents will appreciate the hard work. Perhaps some of your students will want to volunteer for various child-care responsibilities as a result of their service.

Baby-Sitting Service

The cost of baby-sitting is often too expensive for some families in your church and community. Have the students in your church form a baby-sitting pool that provides the service at little or no cost. You may want to provide the baby-sitting service at your church during designated hours. Be sure to provide an adequate adult-to-student-to-child ratio and provide access to a phone for emergencies.

If this is successful with the people in your church, you may want to establish a monthly weekend date night during which the youth group will baby-sit children free of charge. Or offer the service when an adult Bible study, Sunday School class or cell group has a social event or there is an important church business meeting.

Another idea is to provide a Christmas-shopping baby-sitting service on designated weeknights or Saturdays during December to give parents opportunities to do their Christmas shopping.

Provide training for students before having them baby-sit. Many churches have someone—mothers, teachers, nursery attendants, nurses, etc.—who could provide students with the basics of child care, first aid and how to solve problems they might encounter.

Toy Collection

Contact a local organization in your community that collects toys at Christmas or other times during the year for needy children. Organize a toy drive in your church and collect as many toys as possible from the members of your congregation. Instruct the members to bring new unwrapped toys so that the organization can easily identify and distribute appropriate toys to the children.

Another idea is to have the youth group go door-to-door in their neighborhoods and collect good used toys. Make sure the toys are usable or repairable. This can be made

into a contest to see which team can collect the most toys. Be sure to check with the selected organization to make sure they welcome used toys.

Big Brother or Big Sister Ministry

If you have single-parent families in your church, have the young people in your church become big brothers or sisters to the children. It is strongly recommended that you pair up your students and the children in same sex relationships. For example, a senior-high male can become a big brother to an elementary-school-aged boy who is living with his mother. The responsibilities may include meeting them at church, sitting with them in the worship service, calling them during the week, playing ball, going shopping or to other places of interest with them and being available to minister to the family when needed.

Mexican Orphanages

Some of the possible ways to serve in orphanages are to facilitate a Vacation Bible School, day camp or sports camp; build, paint and/or repair facilities; minister through music, puppet and/or drama presentations; or gather and deliver needed supplies, clothing and toys. Rancho de Sus Niños, located in Tecate, Mexico, is one such orphanage. For more information contact: Steve and Cathy Horner; P. O. Box 360; Potrero, CA 91963. Also check with missionaries that your congregation or denomination supports in Mexico.

Missions to the Sick

Hospital Visitation

Get approval through the administration of a local hospital to organize a hospital visitation ministry. Divide students into pairs and have them work a wing or hall of the hospital by visiting those people who would welcome visitors.

The purpose of the visit is to encourage a patient with a brief introduction, light-hearted conversation and a listening ear. Be sure to familiarize your students on proper hospital etiquette such as not leaning or sitting on the patient's bed, talking softly if someone else is resting in the room, maintaining an optimistic attitude and not over-staying your welcome.

Give students some suggestions of topics to talk about such as the students' own interests in sports, hobbies, music, church activities, etc. They can also ask the patients about their interests, their families, their teen years, etc.

Encouragement Ministry

Work with the deacons or helping ministry in your church to put together a list of those who are hospitalized or ill at home in your congregation. Have the students send or deliver cards, flowers, gifts or books to these people. Include prayer for the sick in the church as a regular part of the youth group meeting time. Talk to the patients about their interests, sports, hobbies or music. Pair students with patients who have similar interests. Update the group every week with the progress of patients.

Adopt a Sick Person

This is a great idea for shut-ins in your church who are recovering from surgery or illness or are permanently ill or disabled. Work with the deacons or helping ministry in your church to develop a list of church members recently released from the hospital. With the patient's permission, have groups of two or more in your youth group "adopt" the patient as they recover at home. Adoption can include running errands, preparing meals, cleaning house, writing notes and cards, bringing freshly cut flowers or catching up on chores. If the patients have children, students could baby-sit or visit the children on a regular basis.

Missions to the Hungry and Homeless

Sponsor a Child

There are a number of hunger-relief organizations that welcome help. These organizations allow you to sponsor a child in a third-world country or even in the United States. Sponsorship will assure the child is given food, water, shelter and basic medical care. The organization usually sends the sponsor a picture of the child, brief information about the child and his/her country and an address to send letters to the child.

Once you have decided on an organization, plan a "sponsor a child" event to promote awareness in the group members. Most of the organizations have free video promotionals available to aid in your presentation. The purpose of the event is to educate students on the needs of others around the world and encourage them to sponsor a child for at least one year. Sponsorship of a child usually costs less than a dollar a day. You may want to have the entire group adopt one child or have individual students or small groups of students adopt a child. The trick is to stretch students without over-committing them. Display the sponsored child's picture on a bulletin board and include prayer for the child and letter writing as a regular part of the meeting time.

Visit a Soup Kitchen or Rescue Center

Find a soup kitchen or rescue mission in the phone book, through your community's social service department or through a church network. In some communities, churches band together to provide meals for the down-and-out.

Coordinate students to provide services to the organization according to their needs. Some of the needs may include assistance in preparing and serving meals, sorting and distributing donated clothing, cleaning the facility or presenting a short worship service. If this is a service opportunity that your students enjoy, make it a regular monthly youth group project.

Planned Famine

The idea of a planned famine is to simulate a famine by having students go without food—water and juice is allowed—for a designated period of time, usually about 24 hours. This simulation experience will help students understand in a small way what it feels like to go to bed hungry.

To make your planned famine more meaningful, have people sponsor students by paying them so much an hour for the length of the famine. The money raised by the students can be given to a hunger-relief organization. If possible, hold the famine at the church and use the time to teach students about world hunger, participate in a church or community work project and discuss attitudes toward world hunger. World Vision has a wonderful program called the 30-Hour Famine (see p. 132).

Another variation of this activity is to serve the students a typical "third-world meal" consisting of only rice and tea. Use the meal to illustrate the scarcity of food in third-world countries.

Have a debriefing session after the "famine" to allow students to express their thoughts and concerns and to apply what they learned to their lives.

Food and Clothing Bank

Collect clothes and canned food to be distributed to the poor or homeless in your church or community. This works best if you make it a contest. Divide students into teams and send them out door-to-door to collect as many nonperishable food and clothing items as possible in an hour. The group with the most items wins the contest and a small prize.

Share the list of needs with the whole congregation or even the local community to better serve those in need. With more people involved, more can be helped. The word can be spread through church bulletins and newsletters, posters, newspaper articles, radio/TV announcements, etc. One way that has proven successful for Boy and Girl Scouts, who do this annually, is to announce the upcoming drive in the newspaper a week before the pick-up date, then have groups go door-to-door collecting donations on the designated date.

Once the items of clothing and food are collected, donate them to a rescue mission or community food/clothing bank. Or set up a one-time clothing and food bank at your church.

If you work with an established organization, it is best to contact them ahead of time to make a list of what items they need the most. This is a great service project to use during the holiday season, but don't forget the rest of the year. The needy require help all year, not just at holiday time.

Missions to the Community

Graffiti Busters

If your community has been afflicted with graffiti, organize a work project for the youth group to clean up the mess. Your city may already have a graffiti-removal service. Call the community services department to check. In some cases they will give you the paint, brushes and rollers free of charge and provide a list of places that need painting in your community.

If you decide to organize your own graffiti busters group, check with the home or business owner to receive permission before painting their walls. Some paint and building supply stores may also donate the material needed to clean up your community.

Another good idea is to have your group adopt a residential street, stretch of highway or strip mall and remove graffiti as a year-long project. Check with officials to find out the time commitment and scope of the project.

Adopt a Park

This is a great service project to help beautify your city or town. Because of the rising cost of government, many parks don't get the care and maintenance they need. Select a park near your church and have your group "adopt" it as a regular work project. Adoption can include picking up trash, raking leaves, removing graffiti, cleaning the restrooms, raking sand under the playground equipment and removing weeds. For liability reasons, leave the maintenance of playground equipment to the agency that is responsible for the park. Before you start your project, check with the agency that cares for the park to secure permission.

Public Streets Cleanup

Organize a work project to have the youth group clean up the streets and sidewalks in your neighborhood. Make it enjoyable for students by dividing the group into teams that will compete against each other. Provide each team with a box of trash bags and send them out to pick up as much trash as they can in a two-hour period. For trash to be eligible for the contest it must be found on the ground. Trash found in dumpsters or trash receptacles doesn't count.

After the two-hour period, weigh and total each team's trash bags. The team with the most pounds of trash wins a prize. You may need to rent a dumpster or borrow a few pickup trucks to dispose of the trash at the dump. Recycle collected bottles and cans.

Community Vacation Bible School Program

Organize a community Vacation Bible School program with your youth group and congregation. Your target audience should be needy children who can't afford an expensive program. If you live near a large city, work together with an inner-city church to minister to the needy children in their neighborhood.

To help organize your program, many Christian publishing companies have packaged Vacation Bible School programs that are easily adapted to most situations. These packages come with Bible lessons, games, music, skits and crafts all focused around a central theme. If your own church provides a Vacation Bible School every summer, consider using their materials, decorations, ideas, etc. for this ministry opportunity. Also, enlist the help of adults who are experienced in Vacation Bible School to train and supervise the students.

It is important to provide a low- or no-cost program. Have fund-raisers before the event to offset the cost of supplies and materials. Publicize the event in advance to get congregational support. Ask for donations of materials that will be needed, i.e., craft supplies, snack foods and drinks, etc.

Ministry to Prisoners

Host an Angel Tree Christmas Party for the children and family members of prisoners through Prison Fellowship. It is an opportunity to create a fun atmosphere of games and crafts for the children and to creatively share the gospel. Prior to the Christmas party, the children of prisoners are sponsored and gifts bought in the prisoner parent's name. The gifts are handed out at the end of the party. For more information call Angel Tree at 800-389-HOPE.

Enlist the help of a prison ministry in your community to have briefings for students and adults on the specifics of ministering to families of prisoners. Prepare students ahead of time for what they might see or experience.

Another ministry would be to lead worship services at juvenile hall. Or develop a group of young people and adults to present the gospel message through music, drama and testimonies for a midweek service. There are many resources available that provide worship and drama ideas.

Ministry to Exceptional Children/Adults Homes

Prepare and hold Vacation Bible School at a home for exceptional, abused or disabled children. Prepare a puppet show, skit or drama and perform for the children or adults. Hold a weekly or monthly worship service for the residents. Have students teach crafts, play games or just visit with the residents.

Have someone from the facility come to your youth group meeting to brief students and adult leaders on what they will encounter. Perhaps they could provide a video tape of the programs and residents at the facility to prepare students for what they will experience.

Missions Projects Farther from Home

Native American Reservations

Work projects on a Native American reservation are a wonderful way to expose students to cross-cultural ministry. Work with an established organization to provide Vacation Bible School programs, construction, home repair, door-to-door evangelism or sports ministries. Brief students on what to expect from the residents of the reservation. See resources on pages 127-143.

Construction and/or Work Camp Projects

Construction projects are a great way to introduce students to the concept of service. If you are attempting a construction project on your own, make sure you connect with professional construction workers in your church. The construction workers will need to be involved in every aspect of the project. Never attempt a construction project without the help of professionals.

Contact different members of your congregation, orphanages, camps, children's homes or other churches in the community to find a need. Some possible needs might be clothing, toys, clean-up day, or food bank. Organize a workday or weekend for your group to complete the project.

Organized work camps are another viable option for youth groups. The service opportunities available will vary depending on the organization you choose. Projects include constructing, repairing, cleaning, painting or weatherizing homes, or working in homeless shelters, camps, soup kitchens, inner-city community centers, etc. See list of resources on pages 127-143 and work camps section on pages 113-126.

Disaster Relief

Work with local disaster relief organizations such as the Red Cross, Salvation Army or World Vision to help people affected by disasters. Projects might include organizing blood drives; providing temporary shelter, food or water services; collecting and distributing clothing and/or food; providing basic health care or cleanup crews. Local relief organizations may provide training for such projects.

Inner City Outreach

There are many possibilities to bring God's love to the inner city. If you choose to do this type of ministry, it might work best to link up with a ministry that already ministers in the city such as Youth With A Mission, Center for Student Missions, City Team Ministries, Inner City Impact, etc. (see the resource list beginning on page 127).

Your group could distribute cookies, sandwiches or beverages to street people, telling them of God's love; clean up trash or wash windows; develop drama or music ministries to perform in inner-city parks; or help out at a food/clothing distribution center or soup kitchen.

Habitat for Humanity

Contact Habitat for Humanity International (1-800-HABITAT) for a listing of affiliates in your region or the area to which you are interested in traveling. Once you receive the list, narrow down the possible candidates that fit your criteria. We suggest looking for those chapters that have been in existence for at least 10 years. They usually have a good track record and are well organized, making it a productive week or weekend.

When you contact a Habitat affiliate, ask about: open dates; building plans for the year; supervisors who can guide your group and keep them busy; a daily schedule; tools needed; fees involved; availability of food and housing facilities; orientation provided; time commitment required; climate conditions; and cultural concerns.

Short-Term Mission Trips

Short-term mission trips are the granddaddy of all service projects. A mission trip commands the highest level of commitment. It requires a substantial investment of time and money. A short-term mission project may last anywhere from one week to two or three months. It is best to work with an established mission organization or a seasoned missionary sponsored by your church.

Projects can include constructing homes, churches or other community buildings; evangelizing neighborhoods; providing sports ministries or Vacation Bible School programs; repairing, cleaning or painting homes/churches/church camps; assisting a national church with agriculture training or medical clinics; performing yard maintenance; or working with refugees.

See "The Short-Term Missions Handbook" for detailed information on how to do a short-term mission trip. The list of "Mission and Service Organizations" beginning on page 127 will provide information and addresses for several organizations that provide short-term missions projects.

The Short-Term Missions Handbook

There is no doubt in my mind that a short-term mission trip is one of the greatest opportunities for Christian growth that any student can possibly receive. In these next pages Mike DeVries has put on paper his practical guide for a cross-cultural mission trip. The trip we have chosen to put in this book was an extremely successful youth mission experience that he and his group took to Poland. As you will be able to see, the practical information can translate easily to any part of the world and, with just a little adaptation, you can use much of this material for anything from a nearby work camp to a trip across the world.

Someone once said, "The essence of creativity is the ability to copy." I would only add that the essence of creativity is to copy, then *adapt* to your needs and circumstances. On the following pages we definitely give you permission, in fact we encourage you, to adapt much of the work that Mike and others have done and make your mission trip easier and more effective.

—Jim Burns

Mission Experience Proposal

A year before you actually take your students on almost any mission trip experience, you will want to prepare a one-page mission experience proposal. A mission experience is a large undertaking and you will want the church leadership, parents and students to buy into the vision. The proposal should be prepared 9 to 10 months before the scheduled trip.

Summer Mission Site Proposal

Purpose

The purpose of our mission education program is to provide opportunities for our high school students that will expose them to what God is doing in other cultures, allowing them to be copartners with God in what He's doing all over the world. We believe that when students are placed into situations where their faith is stretched and where they have to trust God more fully, there is life change. Students return home with a vision and a passion for the work of God. This summer we desire to continue our commitment to world missions.

Proposal

In the past, our mission education has focused on places such as the inner city of Los Angeles, Ensenada, Mexico and Guatemala in Central America. Our desire now is to provide our students with something outside the Spanish-speaking world. The following is a proposal for the location of our summer mission project site:

Location: Eastern Europe, Poland (specifically Krakow, Ustron and Wista)
Trip Dates: July 9-22 (tentative)
Team Size: Approximately 30 people
Contacts: Daniel Watts and Waclaw Bylok
Finances: Approximately $1,800 per team member
Pretrip: It will be necessary to take a pretrip sometime in January or February. I'd like to take a couple of staff members along for this trip. Our pretrip should be about six to seven days in length.

Ministry Opportunities

The following are some ministry possibilities for our team to be involved in:

1. Youth camps: outreach
2. Youth and adult conferences: training and equipping
3. Evangelism: outreach
4. Children's ministries: outreach
5. Church ministries: outreach as well as training

Correspondence

The following are sample letters to missionary contacts in Poland and to students and parents. Because it is an international trip, the youth leader will need to take a pretrip. It's better to speak to church leadership, parents and students from firsthand experience.

An information letter written early in the planning stages is important to get families thinking about a trip like this. You need to get information to the parents and students early enough to begin planning and praying about a life-changing trip such as this.

Contact Letter

SAMPLE

To: Waclaw Bylok and Daniel Watts
From: Mike DeVries
        Pastor of High School Ministries

Dear Waclaw and Daniel,

My name is Mike DeVries and I'm the high school pastor at Yorba Linda Friends Church and a ministry associate with the National Institute of Youth Ministry (NIYM). My good friends Jim Burns and Dean Bruns at NIYM suggested I write to you. A couple of weeks ago, I was talking with Jim about possible locations to take a team of high school students for a mission trip. He suggested that I consider taking a team to Poland. I called Dean Bruns and he gave me your names and numbers and told me about the team from Mariner's Church in California that was there last summer.

Last summer we took a team of 20 students and leaders to Guatemala in Central America. We were involved in some fantastic ministry opportunities and had an incredible trip. Next summer, I'd be very interested in bringing a team of high school students to Poland to be involved in what God is doing there. Jim suggested that I begin by contacting you about the possibility of hosting our group next summer. We would love to serve you and minister in any way possible. In the past, we've done evangelism in high schools, construction, children's ministries, church ministries, youth ministries, etc. We'd love to link up with you in any way we can to serve and minister.

The time frame in which we would be able to come to Poland is from July 9 to 22. I will also be available to come to Poland during February to meet you, look at the project and work out the details. One or two other adults will come with me.

Jim and Dean both speak very highly of you and the ministry you have in Poland. I'm very excited about meeting you and possibly serving with you in Poland. Please call or fax me as soon as possible about the possibility of coming next summer so we can begin the planning we would need to do on our end.

May God richly bless your ministry there in Poland!

In Christ,

Mike DeVries
Pastor of High School Ministries

Student and Parent Information Letter

SAMPLE

Dear Parents and High School Students,

Mission trips are unforgettable experiences in which our faith is stretched and our lives changed forever. Mission trips are a hallmark of our high school ministry here at _____(name of church)_____. We've seen God do some incredible things in the lives of high school students who accept the challenge of being a part of one of our many mission project teams. Over the past five years, we've been to many different places, from the inner city of Los Angeles to Ensenada, Mexico and Guatemala in Central America.

Last summer, our team that went to Guatemala was challenged and stretched, returning home with changed lives. If any of you had the opportunity to hear our report from our trip during the Sunday evening service, you saw the impact our students had on the lives of the Guatemalan people, as well as the impact the Guatemalans had on our team members. We're looking forward to seeing the tradition continue.

Next summer, we will be taking a team of high school students and adult leaders to Poland in Eastern Europe. A couple of Sundays ago, I shared about the trip with the high school group and asked them to sign up on an interest list. Your son or daughter signed our list and committed to praying about the possibility of going with us next summer and talking with you about it. We plan on going _____(list dates)_____. Tentatively, we will be involved in ministry to children and teenagers through the schools and camping experiences. The approximate cost for our trip will be $1,800 per person. For our Guatemala trip, we were able to raise the entire amount for our trip, allowing students to go for minimal cost. We will be scheduling opportunities for students to raise money for this trip as well.

I'm excited about the possibilities God has allowed our students to be a part of. I believe that this trip will change the lives of the team members like no other trip has. I'd love for your son or daughter to be a part of this trip. Would you consider talking it over with him or her and praying about it as a family to see if this is an opportunity God would want your teen to be a part of?

After the first of the year, we will be sending an information packet out to those who express an interest in the trip. It will include an information sheet, application and other important information. We will need a commitment sometime in January. In February, I will be traveling to Poland to finalize details with our contacts there. If you have any questions, don't hesitate to call me at the office.

In Christ,

Mike DeVries
Pastor of High School Ministries

Team Organizational Chart and Job Descriptions

One of your first priorities will be to create an organizational chart and a list of job descriptions for each position. This will not only allow the leadership to buy into their part in the trip, it will also let your church leadership and the parents of the students know that you are serious about the responsibilities for this trip. Assigning other responsibilities to team members will help you focus on leading the trip.

Organizational Chart

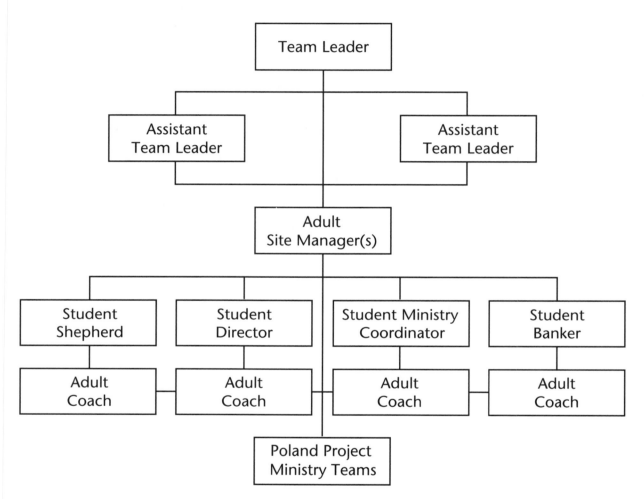

Poland Project Team Job Description

Adult Team Leader

SAMPLE

Primary Functions

1. Administer and lead the Poland Project Team missions experience by providing vision and direction to the Leadership Team.
2. Oversee the training and development of the Poland Project Team as a whole.
3. Ensure that our mission project achieves the mission purpose statement and goals developed by the Leadership Team.

Ministry Reponsibilities

1. Select and oversee the Poland Project Leadership Team, including all areas of vision and direction to the Leadership Team.
2. Oversee the Poland Project Leadership Team meetings, providing the direction for the agenda and the timeline of project completion.
3. Work individually with the Assistant Team Leaders in their role of oversight and direction for the Student Leaders assigned to them.
4. Be the main liaison between the Poland Project Leadership Team and the Site Manager at the ministry site.
5. Be the main liaison between the Poland Project Leadership Team and the church leadership and/or missions leadership of the church.
6. Oversee all training sessions for the Poland Project Team, including vision and direction for training meetings, retreats and field trips.
7. Facilitate the onsite orientation, nightly meetings and debriefing times for the missions experience.
8. Oversee the Poland Project Leadership Team's debriefing dinner.

9. Work with, encourage and support the adult coaches/leaders of the Poland Project Team.

10. Encourage and coordinate plans with the other Poland Project Leadership Team.

11. Attend all Leadership Team Meetings.

12. Commit to praying and planning for the Poland Project Team on a regular basis.

Ministry Qualifications

An adult who possesses the following:

- A deep love for Jesus Christ
- A growing relationship with Him
- A deep love for world missions
- The spiritual gifts of leadership, pastoring and administration
- The gifts of vision, motivation and encouragement
- Experience in a mission setting

Time Commitment

The position of Adult Team Leader will require approximately five to seven hours a week from _____ to _____.
                               (date)   (date)

Supervision

The position of Adult Team Leader will be overseen and supervised by either the youth pastor or church leadership (if the youth pastor is the adult team leader).

Poland Project Team Job Description

SAMPLE

Adult Assistant Team Leaders

Primary Functions

1. Assist in the administration, leadership and development of the Poland Project Team missions experience by working alongside the assigned student leaders.
2. Ensure that our mission project achieves the mission purpose statement and goals developed by the Leadership Team.

Ministry Reponsibilities

1. Assist in the oversight of the Poland Project Leadership Team by overseeing two of the four student leaders—Student Shepherd, Student Ministry Coordinator, Student Director or Student Banker.
2. Assist the student leaders assigned to them through encouragement, support, guidance and direction.
3. Spend time regularly with assigned student leaders to shepherd and pray for them.
4. Assist the Team Leader in overseeing all training sessions.
5. Assist in the facilitation of the on-site orientation, nightly meetings and debriefing times.
6. Encourage, support and work with Adult Coaches/leaders of the Project Team.
7. Encourage and coordinate plans with the other Leadership Team members.
8. Attend all Leadership Team meetings.
9. Commit to praying and planning for the Project Team on a regular basis.

Ministry Qualifications

An adult who possesses the following:

- A deep love for Jesus Christ
- A growing relationship with Him
- A deep love for world missions
- The spiritual gifts of leadership and administration
- The gifts of vision, motivation and encouragement
- Experience in a mission setting

Time Commitment

The position of Adult Assistant Team Leader will require approximately five hours a week from _____ to _____.
                        (date)   (date)

Supervision

The position of Adult Assistant Team Leader will be overseen and supervised by the Adult Team Leader.

Poland Project Team Job Description

Adult Site Manager

SAMPLE

Primary Functions

1. To oversee the on-site administration of the Poland Project Team missions experience while in Poland.
2. Ensure that the mission project achieves the mission purpose statement and goals developed by the Leadership Team.

Ministry Responsibilities

1. Host the Team Leader and Assistant Team Leader(s) for a pretrip to the ministry site, helping to work out the details of the mission experience.
2. Coordinate the following for the Poland Project Team:
   - Ministry site(s)
   - Housing
   - Transportation
   - Orientation
   - Debriefing
   - Training materials that would be beneficial for cultural sensitivity and language training
3. Encourage, support and work with Adult Coaches/leaders of the Project Team.
4. Encourage and coordinate plans with the other Leadership Team members.
5. Commit to praying and planning for the Poland Project Team on a regular basis.

Ministry Qualifications

An adult who possesses the following:

- A deep love for Jesus Christ
- A growing relationship with Him
- A deep love for world missions
- The spiritual gifts of leadership and administration
- The gifts of vision, motivation and encouragement
- Experience in a mission setting

Poland Project Team Job Description

Adult Coaches

SAMPLE

Primary Functions

1. Support, encourage and coach individual team members
2. Serve in any way, shape or form assigned by adult and student team leaders.
3. Ensure that the mission project achieves the mission purpose statement and goals developed by the Leadership Team.

Ministry Responsibilities

1. Encourage and support the team members of the Poland Project Team through the ministry of verbal and written affirmation as directed by the Student Shepherd.
2. Encourage and coordinate plans with the Leadership Team as directed by the adult leaders.
3. Serve in an area of ministry within the trip as directed by the Student Ministry Coordinator.
4. Attend all Leadership Team meetings.
5. Commit to praying and planning for the Project Team on a regular basis.

Ministry Qualifications

An adult who possesses the following:

- A deep love for Jesus Christ
- A growing relationship with Him
- A deep love for world missions
- The spiritual gifts of encouragement, exhortation and service
- Experience in a mission setting

Time Commitment

The position of Adult Coach will require approximately two hours per week in addition to time required by team leaders from _____ to

_____.   (date)

      (date)

Supervision

The position of Adult Coach will be overseen and supervised by the Team Leader and/or Assistant Team Leaders.

Poland Project Team Job Description

Student Banker SAMPLE

Primary Functions

1. Create and administer the budget and financial elements for the Poland Project Team.
2. Assist in creating an environment and experience for mission education to take place during a 14-day trip to Poland in July.
3. Ensure that our mission project achieves the mission purpose statement and goals developed by the Leadership Team.

Ministry Responsibilities

1. Develop and oversee a detailed budget for the Poland Project Team, including all areas of income and expenditures.
2. Oversee and authorize all pretrip expenses in conjunction with the Team Leader.
3. Manage all funds while on-site, keeping records and collecting all receipts.
4. Coordinate plans with and encourage our site managers in Poland.
5. Create and oversee opportunities for the Poland Project Team to raise the necessary funds to achieve our budget, including administration of opportunities, oversight of individual financial accounts and oversight of the corporate financial account.
6. Turn in a complete, detailed written expense report to the Team Leader at the conclusion of the trip, including all incoming money, all expenditures and all receipts.
7. Oversee and work in conjunction with the church financial assistant on the tax exemption verifications for all financial supporters.
8. Maintain regular contact with the missions committee of the church, keeping them updated on all planning and finances.

9. Assist in developing a training format and content, especially relating to the fund-raising and finances of our Poland Project Team.

10. Work with, encourage and support the adult coaches/leaders of the Poland Project Team.

11. Encourage and coordinate plans with the other Poland Project Team Leadership.

12. Attend all Leadership Team Meetings.

13. Commit to praying and planning for the Poland Project Team on a regular basis.

Ministry Qualifications

A high school student who possesses the following:
- A deep love for Jesus Christ
- A growing relationship with Him
- A deep love for world missions
- The spiritual gifts of administration and encouragement
- A detail-oriented person with excellent math skills
- Experience in a mission setting

Time Commitment

The position of Student Banker will require approximately three to four hours per week from _____ to _____.
                           (date)   (date)

Supervision

The position of Student Banker will be overseen and supervised by the Team Leader and Assistant Team Leader.

Poland Project Team
Job Description

Student Director SAMPLE

Primary Functions

1. Direct and facilitate the administrative logistics of the Poland Project Team in an organized manner.
2. Assist in creating an environment and experience for mission education to take place during a 14-day trip to Poland in July.
3. Ensure that our mission project achieves the mission purpose statement and goals developed by the Leadership Team.

Ministry Responsibilities

1. Secure and facilitate all transportation needed for our trip to Poland, including ground and air travel in the U.S. and in Eastern Europe.
2. Coordinate, facilitate and oversee the food and housing for our Project Team while in Poland, in conjunction with our site manager.
3. Coordinate plans with and encourage our site managers in Poland.
4. Develop and coordinate the publicity for the Project Team within the high school ministry and the church as a whole, including T-shirts, banners, flyers, etc.
5. Develop and implement a plan for support, connectedness and partnership with the high school ministry of our church as well as the church as a whole, providing opportunities for involvement such as prayer partners, encouragement system, team commissioning and trip reports.
6. Assist in developing a training format and content, especially relating to the logistics of our Poland Project Team.
7. Work with, encourage and support the adult coaches/leaders of the Poland Project Team.

8. Encourage and coordinate plans with the other Poland Project Team Leadership.

9. Attend all Poland Leadership Team Meetings.

10. Commit to praying and planning for the Poland Project Team on a regular basis.

Ministry Qualifications

A high school student who possesses the following:

- A deep love for Jesus Christ
- A growing relationship with Him
- A deep love for world missions
- The spiritual gifts of administration and leadership
- Experience in a mission setting

Time Commitment

The position of Student Director will require approximately three to four hours per week from _____ to _____.

                       (date)   (date)

Supervision

The position of Student Director will be overseen and supervised by the Team Leader and Assistant Team Leader.

Poland Project Team Job Description

Student Ministry Coordinator

Primary Functions

1. Direct and oversee the ministry and service aspect of the Poland Project Team.
2. Assist in creating an environment and experience for mission education to take place during a 14-day trip to Poland in July.
3. Ensure that our mission project achieves the mission purpose statement and goals developed by the Leadership Team.

Ministry Responsibilities

1. Oversee the planning of all ministry elements of the Poland Project Team, developing a system of ministry teams and supervising all ministry while on-site.
2. Oversee a daily ministry preparation meeting, explaining the ministry for that day—the needs, responsibilities and expectations.
3. Coordinate plans with and encourage our site managers in Poland.
4. Develop and administer several opportunities for the Poland Project Team to serve and minister together as a team before leaving for Poland.
5. Develop a comprehensive plan for continued ministry opportunities for the Poland Project Team in conjunction with the Assistant Team Leader and the Director of Missions and Service.
6. Assist in developing a training format and content, especially relating to the ministry training and preparation of our Poland Project Team.
7. Work with, encourage and support the adult coaches/leadership of the Poland Project Team.

8. Encourage and coordinate plans with the other Poland Project Team Leadership.
9. Attend all Leadership Team Meetings.
10. Commit to praying and planning for the Poland Project Team on a regular basis.

Ministry Qualifications

A high school student who possesses the following:
- A deep love for Jesus Christ
- A growing relationship with Him
- A deep love for world missions
- The spiritual gifts of leadership, service and encouragement
- Experience in a mission setting

Time Commitment

The position of Student Ministry Coordinator will require approximately three to four hours per week from _____ to _____.
                                     (date)   (date)

Supervision

The position of Student Ministry Coordinator will be overseen and supervised by the Team Leader and Assistant Team Leader.

Poland Project Team Job Description

Student Shepherd

SAMPLE

Primary Functions

1. Direct and oversee the spiritual growth, welfare and unity of the Poland Project Team in an organized manner.
2. Assist in creating an environment and experience for mission education to take place during a 14-day trip to Poland in July.
3. Ensure that our mission project achieves the mission purpose statement and goals developed by the Leadership Team.

Ministry Responsibilities

1. Oversee and develop avenues for the Poland Project Team to grow spiritually throughout the selection process, training and mission trip itself such as keeping a journal or diary, worship experiences, guided time with the Lord, etc.
2. Develop and facilitate a nightly debriefing session while in Poland.
3. Coordinate plans with and encourage our site managers in Poland.
4. Develop and implement a plan for the spiritual encouragement/unity within the Poland Project Team such as having prayer partners, sending encouragement notes, etc.
5. Build relationships with the Poland Project Team prior to the trip to nurture spiritual growth and unity.
6. Handle interpersonal problems on the trip in conjunction with the Team Leader.
7. Assist in developing a training format and content, especially relating to the spiritual growth/preparation and team concept of our Poland Project Team.

8. Work with, encourage and support the adult coaches/leadership of the Poland Project Team.
9. Encourage and coordinate plans with the other Poland Project Team Leadership.
10. Attend all Leadership Team Meetings.
11. Commit to praying and planning for the Poland Project Team on a regular basis.

Ministry Organizations

A high school student who possesses the following:
- A deep love for Jesus Christ
- A growing relationship with Him
- A deep love for world missions
- The spiritual gifts of leadership, pastoring and encouragement
- Experience in a mission setting

Time Commitment

The position of Student Shepherd will require approximately three to four hours per week from _____ to _____.
(date)   (date)

Supervision

The position of Student Shepherd will be overseen and supervised by the Team Leader and the Assistant Team Leader.

Developing a Mission Statement

After selecting the Assistant Team Leaders and Student Leaders, begin meeting regularly with them. One of the first things you need to do as a team is develop a mission statement for the mission experience. This statement will describe what you want to accomplish on this mission trip.

The benefits of crafting a mission statement will provide:

- Focus, direction and purpose for the mission experience;
- Parameters for what the trip will, or will not, "look" like;
- Clear and concise goals that team members, parents, church leadership and team leadership will support;
- Credibility for the trip purpose;
- Evaluation points after the trip: Did we accomplish what we set out to do?

Practical Ideas and Possible Hurdles

1. Before writing even one word, PRAY! Pray that God would show you and the leadership team *His* desire and plan for the mission trip.
2. Ask each team leader to write down any ideas, verses or other thoughts resulting from his or her time of prayer.
3. Encourage each team leader to write down a sentence that encapsulates his or her ideas, verses and thoughts about the mission and its purpose.
4. With the entire leadership team, have each person share his or her ideas, verses, thoughts and summarizing sentence.
5. Work together to craft a single sentence that will become the mission statement. You may also want to select a theme verse and title that solidifies the mission statement.
6. Make sure your mission statement is:

    - Clear and concise;
    - Meaningful;
    - Biblical;
    - Compelling and motivating;
    - Memorable and "communicate-able."

The Pretrip

For successful implementation of a cross-cultural missions experience, a pretrip is a must. These next pages include a pretrip itinerary and important questions to have answered about the trip and the resulting report of the pretrip. So much of the success of any missions trip is in the preparation and planning of the experience. The pretrip helps you ask the right questions, meet the people on the mission field and enable you to say to church leadership, parents and students, "My firsthand experience is this..."

Trip Date:	July 21-August 1
Contact:	Daniel Watts (Every Generation Ministries) and Waclaw Bylok
Telephone:	Daniel: 48-122-1-2076 (Poland)
	(719) 260-9690 (Colorado Springs headquarters)
	Waclaw: 48-335-4-2995 (office phone)
	48-335-4-3733 (Fax)
	48-335-5-3588 (private)
Country:	Poland, Eastern Europe
Group Size:	Maximum of 30 people (6 to 7 leaders and 24 students)

Mission Site Inspection

Location

1. What area will we be staying in?

2. What is the population of this area?

3. What is the language spoken in this area?

   Do we need to provide interpreters?

4. What is the political situation in the area?

5. What is the economic status of the people to whom we will be ministering?

6. What is the educational level of the people to whom we will be ministering?

Weather

1. What is the climate usually like on the dates we plan to be there?

2. What is the elevation of the ministry site?

3. Will weather be a factor for our team while we are there? If so, in what ways?

4. What precautions does our team need to follow in regard to the weather?

5. What kind of clothing is recommended for the time we will be there?

Ministry Opportunities

1. What type of ministry will we be doing at the site?

2. What are the age groups of the people that we will be ministering to?

3. If this involves a building project, what does our team need to come prepared to do? What are the building plans, building materials, etc.

4. What skills are needed for our participation in the ministry?

5. What tools or equipment do we need to bring with us?

   What will we need to purchase in the country?

6. What do we need to be aware of when we attempt to clear customs regarding tools, equipment, etc.?

7. Will there be opportunities to preach/share our faith? If so, what group will we be sharing with?

8. What are the most effective vehicles for evangelism for those with whom we will be able to share our faith?

Transportation

1. To what city would our team need to fly?

2. What transportation is available from the airport to the site?

3. How much will transportation cost?

4. What type of transportation will be needed daily to get to the ministry site? How much will it cost?

5. What about transportation back to the airport at the end of our trip?

6. What is the luggage limit, if any?

7. If we need to air freight equipment, what is the best way for us to get equipment to our site?

8. If we need to drive, what are the laws concerning licensing for driving vehicles?

Housing

1. Where will our students be housed?

2. How many beds are available?

3. Will we be paying rent for our housing? If so, how much per person per night?

4. How far will the housing be from the ministry site?

5. Are there sleeping arrangements for married couples? If so, how many couples can be accommodated?

6. Will we need to bring bedding for our team?

7. What are the facilities like where we will be housed?

8. What should/can we bring as gifts for the people we will be staying with?

Food

1. What food is available in the area?

2. Is there additional food available in any areas nearby? If so, where?

   How far away are these areas from our ministry site? From our housing?

3. What food items does our team need to bring with us?

4. What is the average cost in the local restaurants for...

Breakfast?

Lunch?

Dinner?

5. Is there a supermarket, an open market or both nearby?

6. How does the cost of food compare with that in the U.S.?

7. Is there safe drinking water available at the ministry site? At our housing?

8. Is there pure ice available?

9. What utensils, if any, does our team need to bring with us?

10. What are the laundry facilities like?

What does it cost to use the local laundry facilities?

11. Does your mission organization provide a package that includes travel, food and housing? If yes, how much per person?

What does the fee include?

Communication and Safety

1. Is there a telephone where a team member can be reached in case of an emergency? What is the number?

2. Is there a phone nearby from which a team member could call the U.S.? What is the number?

3. Is there a messenger service? If so, what is the name and address of the service?

4. If there is not a phone or a messenger service, how could a team member be reached in case of an emergency?

5. Where is the nearest hospital? What medical services are available?

6. How far is the closest doctor and dentist from the ministry site? From our housing?

7. What are our options if we encounter a medical emergency?

8. What, if anything, do we need to keep in mind for medical concerns?

Entering and Leaving the Country

1. Is a passport required?

2. Is a visa required? If so, where do we secure one?

   What is the cost?

   What documents are required?

3. Which inoculations or vaccinations are required?

   Which are recommended?

4. Is there an airport entrance tax? If so, how much?

   An exit tax? If so, how much?

5. What specific things should NOT be said or done as we come through customs and immigration?

   What *should* be said and done?

6. What should be put on the visa application as the purpose of our trip?

7. What is the location and address that we should put on the visa/tourism card for place of residence while in the country?

Finances

1. What is the name of the local currency?

2. What is the exchange rate between the local currency and the U.S. dollar?

   What do we need to watch for with the exchange rate? Will it be a problem for us on our trip?

   How should we deal with the fluctuation in rates?

3. How should the U.S. dollar be brought into the country: traveler's checks, cash, other?

4. Does the country require each individual to exchange a specified amount of U.S. dollars into local currency at the time of entry into the country? If so, how much?

5. Where is the best place to exchange currency during our trip?

6. Will each individual need to declare the amount of dollars they are carrying at customs and immigration?

7. How will we be paying for expenses: transportation, housing, food, etc.?

Clothing

1. What is the appropriate dress for women: on-site, touring and at church?

2. What things should be worn by women?

   What things should *not* be worn?

3. What is the appropriate dress for men: on-site, touring and at church?

4. What things should be worn by men?

   What things should *not* be worn?

5. What specific cultural sensitivities should the team be aware of related to clothing?

Culture

1. What other cultural sensitivities should our team be aware of?

2. What is the culture of the people we will come in contact with?

3. What is the culture in the other areas that we will be visiting?

4. What cultural elements should we be looking for?

5. What is the spiritual climate of the areas in which we will be?

Sight-Seeing

1. What are the local places of interest?

2. How much does it cost to visit these places?

3. How far away are they from the ministry site?

4. How much would transportation cost to the local points of interest?

5. Are there local stores that sell souvenirs? Any suggestions for local crafts or products to purchase?

6. How does the cost of goods compare with that in the U.S.?

Miscellaneous Questions

1. What specific items could the team bring to help with the local ministry?

2. What specific items could the team bring with which to share their faith?

3. What personal items would you recommend that the team members bring?

4. What personal items would you recommend that the team members *not* bring?

5. How can the team members best prepare themselves spiritually for this project?

6. What should the team members be praying for as they prepare for this project?

Pretrip Report

God is working, moving and changing lives in Poland. Over the seven days that we spent there, we experienced a lot, prayed a lot and grew a lot. Neither of us will be the same. We were impressed with the people, the missionaries whom we met and interacted with, and the ministry that is going on in Poland. I believe that our high school students will have one of the most life-changing and faith-stretching experiences of their lives. They will be challenged and changed. The following report deals with important information regarding our trip.

Itinerary

February 15	Flew to England to meet with Jon and Ruthie Ortlip.
February 16	Landed in London, England. Drove from Manchester to Bolton to see Jon and Ruthie.
February 17	Went with Jon and the Ambassadors in Sport team to a school in Bolton for an outreach event. Over 80 kids showed up for the outreach. Mike shared his testimony.
February 18	Flew from Manchester to London, then London to Warsaw, Poland. Took the train from Warsaw to Krakow.
February 19	Went to church in the morning and evening. Toured parts of Krakow for the rest of the day.
February 20	Spent the day sightseeing and touring around Krakow.
February 21	Met with the Every Generation Ministries (EGM) staff to discuss our ministry for the summer. Spent the majority of the day traveling to southern Poland to see a possible camp/ministry site for our team in July.
February 22	Met with the EGM staff. Went sightseeing and touring around Krakow, Wawel Castle and Wieliczka.
February 23	Met with the EGM staff. Spent the rest of the day at Auschwitz-Birkenau.
February 24	Traveled by train from Krakow to Warsaw in preparation for flight home.
February 25	Flew from Warsaw to London, then London to New York and New York to Los Angeles.

The People of Poland

The people of Poland were absolutely wonderful. They were warm, inviting and very hospitable. They were very open to Americans and very kind. There is a deep spiritual hunger among the people of Poland. They are a strong-willed people, standing up under the rule of both Nazi Germany and the communist Soviet Union. They are intensely nationalistic, yet open to the West. Their history and culture is steeped in Catholicism.

Under German occupation, the Polish language was outlawed in public. The Polish people had to retreat into the Roman Catholic Church to be able to speak Polish and be Polish. Under communist rule, the Polish culture was the target for destruction. The people once again retreated to the Catholic Church to exercise their cultural heritage and continue to "be Polish." At that time, over 85 percent of the country was involved in the Catholic Church. Since the fall of communism, involvement in the Catholic Church has plummeted. Currently, about 10 percent of the population is involved in the Catholic Church. As for Protestantism, it is even worse—only 4 out of every 1,000 people are involved in a Protestant church.

There is a great need for the Polish people to hear about the love of Christ and the relationship we can have with Him! Poland is a harvest field ready and ripe for the gospel. Eastern Europe as a whole is a fertile ground for the gospel of Christ. I believe that this will be an incredible opportunity for our students to:

1. See God at work in a culture radically different from their own;
2. Be used of God to meet needs and share the love of Jesus Christ;
3. Be challenged and changed for a lifetime.

Every Generation Ministries

We were equally impressed with the ministry with which we will be involved—Every Generation Ministries (EGM). They are a mixed group of Americans and Poles focused on the same goals: proclaiming Christ and training leaders in Poland. EGM's purpose and vision is multifaceted. They exist to:

1. Translate and publish Christian literature for children's, youth and overall church ministries into Polish to support the Christian leadership in Poland.
2. Train children's and youth workers on a national level, equipping Polish leaders to do ministry.
3. Be a link between Polish ministries and short-term adult and youth missionaries from the United States.
4. Offer short-term missionary and/or leadership internships for those interested in ministering in Eastern Europe.

I'm excited, not only about the possibilities for this summer with our students, but about a future relationship with this ministry on youth and adult levels for missions/ministry. EGM has an incredible ministry with great leadership and vision. They are also currently working on multiplying this ministry in St. Petersburg, Russia.

Summer Ministry

For our trip we will be in Poland for three weeks from July 12 to August 1. We will be involved in a children's camp in the northern Polish community of Narewka. The particulars are:

Trip Dates: July 12 to August 1

July 12 to July 15—Travel, acclimation, orientation and sight-seeing

July 16 to July 29—Camp in Narewka

July 30 to August 1—Debriefing and sight-seeing, travel home

Team Size: Approximately 15 to 20 people

Ministry

Our students will be assisting at a two-week children's camp for 7 to 12 year olds. They will be involved in the following:

- Leading small group discussions on a daily basis;
- Leading small group activities;
- Teaching and presenting evangelistic and growth-oriented dramas;
- Overseeing a nightly fellowship time that will include games, music, drama and testimonies;
- Planning an outreach event for the community on the next-to-last night of the camp;
- Planning and leading a worship service in the local church of Narewka on Sunday morning.

Conclusion

I believe that this trip will be one of the most incredible experiences and learning opportunities our high school students have ever had. They will be challenged, changed and

stretched in incredible ways. They will experience and see things and minister in ways they never have before. For some it may be a vocational calling point, for others it may be something that changes their perspective on God, but all will return changed. The people of Poland are hungry for the gospel and for a relationship with God. I'm excited about seeing our students be a part of building the kingdom of God.

The Budget

Obviously you'll need an extensive budget for any mission experience. The length of the stay and the traveling distance dramatically affect the budget. We've included Mike's basic budget to help you create your own. Experience tells us that you'll need more money than you plan for the little emergencies that come along the way. This requires a larger-than-usual miscellaneous budget item.

Mission Trip Budget

Area	Description	Budgeted Amount	Actual Costs
Air Travel	Team Poland round-trip from U.S. to Poland	$17,392.15	$17,392.15
Room and Board	Lodging and meals ($15 per day x 21 days = $315 per person)	$5,355.00	$5,355.00
	Camp costs ($100 per team member x 17 days)	$1,700.00	$1,700.00
Ground Transportation	Round-trip train from Warsaw to Krakow	$765.00	$765.00
	Round-trip bus from Krakow to Narewka	$425.00	$425.00
	Vans to L.A. airport ($75 per van x 3 vans)	$225.00	$225.00
Training	Holocaust Museum tour	$100.00	$100.00
	Ropes Course visit	$629.00	$555.00
	Guest speaker (3 speakers x $75 each)	$225.00	$225.00
	Binders and dividers for team	$200.00	$121.65
Administration	Pretrip expenses	$3,000.00	$4,363.30
	Fund-raising start-up costs	$700.00	$770.53
	Hats	$432.00	$432.00
	Small banks	$100.00	0
	Books, videos, maps, lunches	$200.00	$193.91
	Mailing costs	$300.00	$64.00
	Banners	$250.00	$125.00
	Phone and fax to Poland	?	

Area	Description	Budgeted Amount	Actual Costs
Ministry Equipment	Duffel bags	$100.00	$170.00
	Drama makeup	$100.00	$100.00
	Recreation equipment	$100.00	$100.00
	Medical kits—one for Team Poland & one for camp	$100.00	$100.00
Miscellaneous	Film and developing	$400.00	$214.25
	Miscellaneous	$1,201.85	$311.64
Totals		**$34,000.00**	**$33,808.43**

Applications, Evaluations and References

We've included the following applications, references, evaluations and all the other important forms needed for a mission trip so that you can easily adapt them to your situation.

Team Member Application

SAMPLE

Shining Out the Light, Piercing the Darkness

Thanks for being interested in shining out the light as a part of TEAM POLAND. God is going to do some absolutely radical things in and through us as we allow Him to use us to minister to the people of Poland. This trip is designed to be an intense, short-term, overseas mission project. The following application is designed for you to evaluate your interest in serving Christ this summer for 14 days in Poland. It is also designed for us to get to know you a little better, to hear your heart and hear what God has been doing in your life. Please take the time to prayerfully complete this application and return it to us as soon as possible because space is limited on this trip.

    This application is the first step in becoming a part of our 30-member TEAM POLAND. Once you have filled out your application and have two sealed evaluations completed by two adults, return the packet to the church office no later than _____.

                                                           (date due)

Name _____   Birthdate _____

Address _____

_____

Phone _____

School _____Grade this fall _____

Spiritual Background

1. In a brief paragraph, describe how you came to have a relationship with Jesus Christ.

2. What has God been doing lately in your life?

   What has He been teaching you?

   How has He been challenging you?

3. In what areas of the high school ministry have you been involved?

   In what areas of church or other ministries have you been involved?

4. In your own words, what do you think it means to be in love with Jesus Christ?

5. If someone were to ask you what it means to have a relationship with Christ and how he or she could have one, what would you say?

6. What is the most difficult or most challenging thing that you have ever done? What made it so challenging or difficult?

7. What do you do to keep close to God in your relationship with Him and maintain your personal growth with Christ?

Ministry Background

1. What other mission/service projects have you been involved with?

What are some of the ministries you were involved in as a part of those projects?

2. Have you ever had any experience in sharing your faith, drama ministry or being involved in worship services? If so, what?

3. Have you ever been involved in any other areas of ministry? If so, what?

Team Information

1. Why do you want to be a part of this trip?

2. What are some of your expectations, fears and apprehensions about going to Poland to serve?

3. What do you think are some of your strengths, abilities, gifts or experiences that would be a benefit to our trip?

4. The mission statement for our trip states that we are going "to serve and love the people of Poland, ministering as Jesus would, in His power; and proclaiming the life-changing message of His love through our relationships and our lives." What does this mean to you? What will you do as a part of TEAM POLAND to make this happen?

5. A few of the most important qualities for our team are encouragement, unity and servanthood. What do these mean to you? What will you do to make these qualities a part of our team?

    Encouragement

    Unity

    Servanthood

Team Commitment and Covenant

SAMPLE

Shining Out the Light, Piercing the Darkness

1. Do you agree to attend all of the training sessions prior to our departure for Poland?

2. Do you agree to complete all the training assignments prior to our departure for Poland?

3. Will you keep a journal while on our trip, describing our trip and how God has been teaching and challenging you while on the trip?

Read the following statements, then sign and date.

I realize that being a part of TEAM POLAND is a responsibility as well as a privilege. I realize that I will be expected to...

- Be a part of a team.
- Have a positive attitude in all circumstances.
- Be an ambassador of the United States,_____,
  and, most importantly, Jesus Christ.   (name of church)
- Obey all directions given by team leadership and our hosts.
- Have a Christlike character in all situations.
- Be a servant and encourager.
- Strive to be culturally sensitive to the Polish culture at all times while in Poland.

Student _____ Date _____

Parent/Guardian _____ Date _____

Received by _____ Date _____

Team Member Reference

Thank you for taking the time to complete this reference form for one of our students. During the summer, we are planning to take 30 people to Poland for 14 days of mission education. They will be involved in various service projects and ministry opportunities while we are there. This student selected you as one of two references. Please take a moment to share with us your thoughts about this student. Your honest input is extremely important to us as we select our team for this trip. After you have filled out this evaluation, seal it in the attached envelope and give it to the student or drop it in the mail to us. Once again, thank you for your help!

Student _____ Date _____

1. What is your relationship with the student and how long have you known him/her?

2. What is your impression of the student? What are five words that you would use to describe him or her?

3. What strengths does this student have that will positively impact this mission project?

4. Are there any weaknesses that may affect this student's ability to make a positive contribution to this mission project? Please explain.

5. On a scale of 1 to 5, with 5 being the highest, how would you rate the student in the following areas? Please explain each rating.

   _____   Works well with others

   _____   Leadership ability

   _____   Reliability

   _____   Motivation

   _____   Disposition

   _____   Emotional stability

   _____   Concern for others

6. Please make any additional relevant comments regarding this student.

Signed _____ Date _____

Phone _____

Team Member Evaluation SAMPLE

This evaluation is VERY important to us! Your responses will help shape future international mission trips coming from our ministry. Please take time and thought in responding to ALL the questions on this evaluation.

Team Member _____

1. Rate each of the following elements on a scale of 1 to 5 (1 = needs work for next trip and 5 = incredibly great, keep it!) and include any comments that would help explain your rating.

1   2   3   4   5   a. Did the trip provide a realistic missions experience?

1   2   3   4   5   b. Do you think TEAM POLAND made a difference in the lives of the Polish people?

1   2   3   4   5   c. Do you feel that you made an impact?

1   2   3   4   5   d. Food

1   2   3   4   5   e. Housing

1   2   3   4   5   f. Camp ministry as a whole

1   2   3   4   5   g. Drama ministry

1   2   3   4   5   h. Evening fellowship times with the campers

1   2   3   4   5   i. Community outreach in Narewka

1   2   3   4   5   j. Site Managers, Jeff and Ania

1   2   3   4   5   k. Trip leadership

1   2   3   4   5   l. Sight-seeing while in Poland

1   2   3   4   5   m. Encouragement system

1   2   3   4   5   n. Training for the trip

1   2   3   4   5   o. Spiritual preparation for the trip

1   2   3   4   5   p. Schedule while in Poland

1   2   3   4   5   q. Length of the trip

1   2   3   4   5   r. Spiritual impact of the trip

1   2   3   4   5   s. Overall experience

1   2   3   4   5   t. Other _____

2. What surprised you the most about the people of Poland?

3. What "stone of remembrance" have you taken with you from this trip?

4. What was the most positive aspect of our trip to Poland?

5. What was the least positive aspect of our trip to Poland?

6. What are two things that you learned about...

God?

Our team?

Yourself?

7. How was your experience as a member of TEAM POLAND?

8. How can we improve...

Publicity/promotion of the trip?

Team building?

Training?

Fund-raising?

9. How else can we improve the experience for future international mission trips?

10. How is your life going to be different when you return home?

11. How are you planning to "keep the fire alive"?

12. Would you participate in another mission trip? Explain.

13. Would you be interested in being a part of the leadership of future mission trips?

Training Schedules and Itineraries

The following pages contain samples of training and daily schedules and a sample of the itinerary for the whole trip.

Training Schedule

March 26th—Orientation

"Getting to Know Ya"
Trip Orientation
Dates and Deadlines
Passport and inoculation info to TEAM

April 9th—Parent Information Meeting

Pretrip slide/video show
Fund-raising plan
Ministry plan
Administration
- Hand out medical release forms
- Information table sign-ups
- Frequent Flyer number
Prayer

April 23rd—Training Session One

Worship
Challenge/memory verse
Ministry training
- Drama training
- Rehearse "Hands" and "She Gave Her Heart Away"
Administration
- Medical release forms due
- Proof of overseas health insurance due
- Give out TEAM T-shirts
- Take TEAM picture for prayer calendar
- Information table sign-ups
- Hand out journal assignment one
- Hand out reading list
Devotion/journaling: Time with God
Support-letter names and personal paragraph
Group prayer and with prayer partners

April 30th—Training Session Two

Worship
Team-building exercise
Challenge/memory verse
Ministry training
- Testimony training: Why and how to share your faith

Fund-raising
- Individualized letters
- Support-letter materials

Spiritual preparation
- Journal assignment two
- Devotion/journaling: Time with God

Administration
- Binders

Prayer

May 7th—Training Session Three

Cultural training
- Visit Holocaust Museum in Los Angeles

Fund-raising
- Bulk mailing of support letters

Prayer

May 21st—Training Session Four

Worship
Team-building exercise
"Ministry in Poland" with Bob Webster
Memory verse
Ministry training
- Testimony training
- Drama training

Fund-raising update
Administration
- Hand out packing list

Prayer

May 28th—Training Session Five

Worship
Challenge/memory verse
Ministry training
- Drama training
- Testimony training

Fund-raising update
Prayer

June 4th—Training Session Six

Worship
Challenge/memory verse
Ministry training
- Drama training
- Camp ministry training

Cultural training
- Language training

Fund-raising update
Administration
- Inoculation deadline
- Passport deadline

Prayer

June 11th—Training Session Seven

Worship
Challenge/memory verse
Ministry training
- "How to Work with Kids" with Dianna Urey
- Drama training
- Camp ministry training

Fund-raising update
Prayer
Set up for BASIX concert
TEAM POLAND Benefit Concert with BASIX from 6:00 P.M. to 7:30 P.M.

June 17th—Training Session Eight

Team-building exercises
Ropes course, 8:00 A.M. to 5:00 P.M.

June 28th—Training Session Nine

Drama training and refinement, 9:00 A.M. to 1:00 P.M.

July 1st—Training Session Ten

Drama training and refinement, 9:00 A.M. to 1:00 P.M.

July 2nd—Training Session Eleven

Worship
Challenge/memory verse
Ministry training
- Camp ministry training

Cultural training
- Language training

Administration
- Hand out TEAM duffel bags
- Hand out journal assignment three

Fund-raising update
Prayer

July 9th—TEAM Commissioning Service

All three morning services

July 9th—Training Session Twelve

Worship
Overflow training
Administration
- All money due by July 7

Prayer
Send-off dinner from 6:00 P.M. to 8:30 P.M.

Trip Itinerary

SAMPLE

July 12

9:00 A.M.	Meet at the church
9:30 A.M.	Pick up by airport shuttle
10:30 A.M.	Arrive at LAX for check-in
1:30 P.M.	Depart LAX on Delta flight #58. Change planes in Frankfurt, Germany

July 13

2:10 P.M.	Arrive at Warsaw International Airport, Poland
4:00 P.M.	Catch train bound for Krakow
6:30 P.M.	Arrive at Krakow, Poland
	Eat dinner
	Relax and sleep

July 14

_____	Morning briefing session
_____	Sight-seeing in Krakow
_____	Lunch
_____	Sight-seeing in Krakow
_____	Dinner
_____	Evening briefing session

July 15

_____	Morning briefing session
_____	Depart by bus for Narewka

July 16—July 29

_____	Camp work in Narewka (see camp schedules for specifics)

July 23

_____	Church service in the community of Narewka

July 28

_____   Community outreach in Narewka

July 29

_____   Return to Krakow by bus

July 30

_____   Debrief and sightsee at Auschwitz-Birkenau

July 31

_____   Debrief and sightsee at the Wieliczka Salt Mine

August 1

_____   Debrief and sightsee

August 2

6:30 A.M.   Arrive at Warsaw International Airport for check-in
8:20 A.M.   Depart Warsaw International Airport on Delta flight #57. Change planes in Frankfurt, Germany
2:00 P.M.   Arrive at LAX

Daily Camp Schedule

SAMPLE

7:30 A.M.	Staff fellowship time
8:00 A.M.	Wake up
8:30 A.M.	Group fellowship time
9:00 A.M.	Breakfast
9:30 A.M.	Clean up sleeping areas
10:00 A.M.	Trip/activity
2:00 P.M.	Dinner
2:30 P.M.	Quiet time
3:15 P.M.	Bible lesson for younger children Activity for older children
4:15 P.M.	Snack
4:45 P.M.	Bible lesson for older children Activity for younger children
6:00 P.M.	Supper
7:00 P.M.	Evening fellowship time
8:30 P.M.	Prepare for bed
9:30 P.M	Bedtime for children
9:30 P.M.	Evening debrief for TEAM POLAND
10:30 P.M.	Bedtime

Guidelines and Information

The following pages contain samples of the guidelines for safety, courtesy and behavior standards for the trip and the vital information each participant needs regarding requirements, deadlines and costs of the trip.

Trip Guidelines

Please keep in mind that in everything you say and everything you do, you are representing our high school ministry, _____(name of church)_____, our country and Jesus Christ Himself. This cannot be stressed enough. While you are in Poland, you are invited guests and need to act with respect and honor toward others. The following are guidelines for our trip to Poland:

While Clearing Immigration and Customs

- Always be polite and respectful to agents in Poland and the United States.
- Please do not joke around or be loud.
- Answer all the questions that are asked of you.
- Be sure to have your passport and any other paperwork ready at all times while clearing immigration and customs.

While in Poland

- Always be polite and respectful to any person you may encounter in Poland.
- Obey any direction given to you by those in authority.
- Please do not be loud or obnoxious.
- Please, no "couples" on the trip.
- Please do not make fun of or joke about either the Polish people or their culture.
- Don't make comments in English, thinking others won't understand you, because they might.
- Think before you speak!
- Don't come with a "superior" attitude toward the Polish culture.
- Don't be afraid to be a learner—ask questions!
- Try to speak the language.
- Allow yourself to be inconvenienced—and expect it!
- Always expect the need for flexibility and change.
- Always ask yourself the question: "What would Jesus do?"

While in Narewka

- As you lift up Christ, don't put down the Roman Catholic Church. Don't debate the differences. Focus on a personal faith in Jesus Christ.
- Share as much of yourself as possible with the children.

- Give 100 percent of yourself every day in every way.
- Keep your focus on the children at the camp and not on each other.

As a Part of the TEAM

- Always be an encourager.
- Always pray for each other.
- Always resolve conflicts with each other.
- Always love one another.
- Always be an example in speech, in life, in love, in faith and in purity (see 1 Timothy 4:12).

I have read and I understand these trip guidelines. I agree to follow these guidelines.

Signed _____ Date _____

Team Member Info Sheet

SAMPLE

Dates: July

We are currently looking at the second and third weeks or the third and fourth weeks: July 9 through 23 or July 16 through 30. The dates will be finalized in the next two weeks.

Location: Krakow, Poland

Ministry

We will be involved in the following ministries:
- Camp ministries
- Children's ministries
- Evangelism
- Drama ministries
- Ministering in hospitals/prisons (possibly)

Cost: Approximately $1,800 Per Person

The final cost will be set by _____(date)_____. There could be a possible fluctuation up or down, but not much. We will be doing fund-raising as a team as well as having opportunities for students to raise individual funds.

Commitment

To be a part of TEAM POLAND, team members will be asked to:
- Commit to following our team covenant;
- Attend all training meetings for our team;
- Complete all training assignments;
- Be involved in fund-raising for our trip—each student is ultimately financially responsible.

Application Process

If you're interested in being a part of this missions education experience, you need to do the following:

1. Pick up an application packet.
2. Fill out the application and return it to _____ (name) _____ by _____ (date) _____ .
3. Have two adults fill out the reference forms and return them to the church in the envelopes provided no later than _____ (date) _____ .

Mission Trip Flowchart

Every mission trip needs a flowchart. The following chart covers most of the details of any mission trip, but obviously you will need to adapt it to meet your needs.

Mission Trip Flowchart

SAMPLE

Weeks out from trip	Date completed	Person in charge	
			Pretrip Plans
			Write trip proposal.
			Write trip mission statement and goals.
			Write letter to possible site hosts.
			Obtain approval from missions committee.
			Develop organizational chart.
			Develop leadership job descriptions.
			Create a pretrip report.
			Decide on a trip theme.
			Select trip theme verse.
			Finances
			Develop a budget.
			Get budget approval.
			Develop a fund-raising plan and timeline.
			Implement fund-raising plans.
			Prepare financial pretrip report.
			Prepare financial posttrip report.
			Communication
			Pass around interest sign-up sheet to students.
			Write letter to interested parents and students.
			Develop a prayer calendar.
			Informational meeting for parents.
			Create a parent information sheet.

Weeks out from trip	Date completed	Person in charge	
			Publicity
			Create trip artwork & logo.
			Shirt and logo samples to leadership.
			Order TEAM T-shirts.
			Develop information booth plans.
			Schedule TEAM members to work at information booth.
			Design a trip banner.
			Administration
			Give site inspection report to leadership.
			Send site inspection report to site host.
			Give passport information to TEAM.
			Set passport mailing deadline.
			Make passport reminder calls.
			Give overseas health information to TEAM.
			Hand out medical release forms to TEAM.
			Medical releases and inoculations completed.
			Create a "What to bring" list.
			Send "What to bring" list to TEAM.
			Scheduling
			Create a trip planning timeline.
			Create leadership team meeting schedule.
			Create trip itinerary and schedule.
			Transportation
			Make preliminary airline reservations.
			Finalize airline reservations.
			Make U.S. transportation arrangements.
			Finalize U.S. transportation plans.
			Housing
			Contact trip site for housing plans.
			Communicate budget issues.
			Create "What to bring" list.

Weeks out from trip	Date completed	Person in charge	
			Equipment
			Create ministry equipment list.
			Create travel equipment list.
			Church Involvement
			Enlist congregational prayer partners.
			Have sign-ups for parent involvement.
			Schedule send-off dinner.
			Schedule church prayer and commissioning service.
			TEAM Training
			Give applications to TEAM members.
			Applications due back.
			Create a final list of all TEAM members.
			Schedule training dates.
			Prepare slide/video show of pretrip visit.
			Give training ideas and contents to leadership.
			Order training materials.
			Plan Training Session One.
			Plan Training Session Two.
			Plan Training Session Three.
			Plan Training Session Four.
			Plan Training Session Five.
			Plan Training Session Six.
			Plan Training Session Seven.
			Schedule guest speakers.
			Schedule TEAM interviews.
			Adult Coaches
			Give adult coach job descriptions to leadership.
			Select possible coaches.
			Make initial contact to possible coaches.
			Finalize confirmation of coaches.

Weeks out from trip	Date completed	Person in charge	
			Ministry
			Develop ministry area lists.
			Sign-up list for TEAM members.
			Schedule team ministry training.
			TEAM Spiritual Development
			Prepare journal materials.
			Prepare Bible study materials.
			Prepare team binders.
			Implement encouragement system.
			Prepare prayer calendar.
			Posttrip Events
			Review trip evaluations.
			Give evaluations to mission committee.
			Debrief the trip with the TEAM.
			Write a church report.
			Finalize all budget and logistical issues.
			Send thank-you letters to all leadership.
			Start planning next trip.

Work Camps

Scott attended our work camps just about every summer. From Maine to Mississippi and just about anywhere else we ventured, Scott made sure he was part of every work camp. In college his background in work-camp experiences led him to become active in a university program that helped others. He later became a leader of the group. This earned him the coveted President's Award in his senior year. He's at seminary now studying to be a pastor and still helping others through volunteering. Each summer, he makes plans to come home and join us on work camp as an advisor.

Gretchen's story is much the same. She always attended work camp in high school and signed up each year after graduation. She's in school in New York City, but she manages to plan summer classes and work around our week of helping others. She's leading the kids now as a chaperone and doing something concrete with her faith by helping to change the living conditions of some of God's most needy.

There are others. Many others. Each student was an ordinary youth group member who took the challenge and worked to raise money to work on the homes of other people. Sometimes the participants lived in homes that were not much better than those we were repairing or painting, but they never spoke a critical word. They immersed themselves in the work efforts with spirit and devotion; a reflection of the relationship they enjoyed in Christ. Many have gone into ministry of one kind or another. Many found deeper faith in Christ through the love and accomplishment of a work-camp experience. And your group can, too.

Matthew 25:31-46 extends to us the responsibility of reaching out to our world to make a difference in the name of Jesus. Whether it's a soup kitchen, a house-building organization or an agency touching the lives of the hurting, our churches are called to reach out in the name of Jesus Christ. It is in this same spirit that work camps provide immeasurable blessing to both the recipient of the labors and youth group members as well.

Why Work Camps?

The "why" of work camps is not a short, simple answer. It involves many aspects of our Christian experience and commitment. To briefly indicate a few, work camps…

- Provide a strong, personal mission experience consistent with Scripture.
- Build a level of community within the group that is unmatched by most other endeavors.
- Involve teens in leadership training that builds self-esteem and rapport among the group.
- Give the leaders and the group a chunk of time that is isolated and insulated from the real world to create a sense of Christian community that cements relationships through the accomplishment of a common goal.
- Develop helping skills among members that most of them do not have: painting, carpentry, construction, etc.
- Are enormously fun and give an unmatched adventure in modern society.
- Remind students how blessed they are, how needy others can be and that something can really be done to make a difference in the lives of others.

The Blessing of Work Camps

Each camp is so unique, so different that no one can map it out completely for you. However, these ideas and suggestions will help you in putting together a work camp that can change lives, both within your group and in the people you help, and teach teenagers that they can make a difference. So, what are you waiting for? Get planning! Your group will never be the same, and Christ's love will be exhibited to a hurting and needy part of this world.

The Process

If you've never planned or attended a work camp, the prospect can seem overwhelming. How do I begin? Where do I start? What are the steps involved?

The process is multifaceted and, at times, rather complex. Each of these areas is important in building a great camp experience. The steps to a successful work-camp program are explained on the following pages.

Convincing the Youth Group

It is not unusual to have this great idea, "This summer I'll take the kids to a work camp!" only to find the idea greeted with no enthusiasm. There is a reason for this. Students today tend to be self-indulgent and self-centered, just as is society in general. The "I'm Number One" and "Me First" way of life is pervasive in our society, in direct opposition to the purposes of work camping. However, if the idea is introduced slowly, with a couple of programs or studies preceding the proposal, you'll find fertile ground for the idea. Often, when students have not experienced something, they assume it is no good.

☛ Bring in adult and student leaders from a group that has had a successful work camp. Let them tell their story, and then sit back and enjoy the response from your students.

Persuading the Church Board

☛ Convince the students, get the support of parents, then request that the board hear your proposal. Take representatives from each group involved in the process: students, parents and youth leaders.
☛ Include as many specifics as possible in the proposal:
  • Itinerary,
  • Budget,
  • How many students would go,
  • What each one would contribute to his or her support,
  • Parent support,
  • Chaperones,
  • Letters from the organization sponsoring the work camp,
  • Requirements on your time,
  • Type of work to be done,
  • Who will be helped—needy, elderly, etc.
☛ Go into the meeting with enthusiasm, not with fear of defeat.
☛ Be prepared; don't overlook insurance limitations, transportation problems, timing or money.

- After the presentation/discussion, ask the board to bless the endeavor.
- If they catch you in a blind spot, be gracious, ask that the request be tabled and get the information they need.
- If the board is willing, ask that a board member be assigned to work with you in working out the details. Then it becomes part of the board's work and not just an additional item of business.

Enlisting Students

- Enlist early. Start talking about next year's work camp at the end of this year's camp. "Striking while the iron is hot" creates strong affiliation for next year's camp as you are coming off of the high of this year's experience.
- Provide students and their families with plenty of notice for the destination, dates and details of work camp.
- The best advertisers are students who have gone on a work camp before. Adding adventure to the work camp enhances it even more.
- Begin signing up students as soon as possible—right after returning home from work camp.
- If this is your first attempt, gain momentum in small steps, one teen at a time, to fill the spots in a small camp.
- Plan a camp that is mostly work, but also offers significant fun and adventure time. If you start with a smaller camp at first, the following years will take care of themselves.

Selecting a Work Camp Site

- Check your denomination's missions office for possible work camp sites.
- Check the missions your church sponsors to see if one of the missionaries, agencies, or groups your local church supports regularly has any work needing to be done.
- If a natural disaster has occurred, write to churches in the area to see if you might bring a group to help.
- Call churches in your area who have gone on work camps and ask them for some suggestions.
- Ask around if anyone within your congregation might know of an organization or place in need.

After you have found some possible locations:

- Ask your student leaders to begin contacting possible locations or organizations for information.
- Hold a work-camp interest planning meeting and let each leader share what she or he discovered.

☞ Pick two possible sites with a third for standby, and begin to figure out details. A standby is essential—in case you reach a dead end and discover too little time is available to work out another plan.

Raising the Funds

We charge each student $100 to participate in the work camp, and I never ask adult volunteers to pay. The camps usually cost about $4,000 or more. We usually take about 25 students to each work camp. The registration brings in about $2,500, so we need to generate an additional $2,000.

To make fund-raising as painless as possible, we use a number of annual fund-raisers that bring in good bucks and are fairly easy to manage. For example:

- For Christmas and Easter we sell poinsettia and lily plants, respectively, for $10 apiece. We pay $3 for each plant and bank $7. To make these even more attractive to the congregation, we print a special page in our bulletin which gives the buyer the option to buy the flower "In Honor of..." or "In Memory of...." The plants are displayed in the worship service the Sunday before Christmas and on Easter Sunday.
- For Valentine's Day we offer a dozen carnations delivered to any address within a 15-mile radius of the church for $10. We buy them for around $4 a dozen and make $6 per sale.
- Sell stock at $10.00 per share to encourage church members to invest in the lives of the students. These are pure profit dollars as there is only the printing of the certificate, which we do on our church copier.

Stay away from fund-raisers that reap low profits and take lots of time to organize such as car washes, bake sales, etc. We do offer a couple of meals, but for other reasons:

- Building important rapport with the church leadership if they need a meal for a church gathering, such as the annual church business meeting.
- Students get to work together for a short-term goal which builds relationships for the week at work camp.

☞ Another option is to raise the registration fee to $125 or to budget a line item in your youth budget for work camps.

Building Pretrip Community

☞ Hold a number of mandatory pretrip meetings to get the students acquainted with one another.
☞ Prayer times, fund-raisers, planning teams for the work camp and other meetings are also team-building opportunities.

☞ Blending the group before the trip will help to insure that the trip is successful.

Monitoring Registration Money

☞ Some families will need to make payments over several months. Allowing families to make payments will be appreciated and assure that low-income kids have an opportunity to join the group.

☞ Ask an organized parent to keep the books and communicate with the families.

The Packing List

Keep the list as simple as possible. Strive for a lean-and-mean work camp with as little equipment as reasonably possible. A sample packing list:

- ❏ Enough work and casual clothes for the week
- ❏ Medications (adult leaders should know what they are)
- ❏ One or two dress outfits for church attendance or a day off
- ❏ Bible, notebook, pens or pencils
- ❏ Comfortable work and leisure shoes
- ❏ Work gloves and eye protection
- ❏ Sleeping bag, pillow and optional air mattress
- ❏ Towel, washcloth and toiletries
- ❏ Reading material, small games
- ❏ Tools: hammer, regular and Phillips screwdrivers, cloth nail belt, paint brushes, scrapers, etc. to fit the specific needs of the work camp
- ❏ Extra socks and underwear (enough to make it through the week without doing laundry)
- ❏ Rain gear, swimsuit, jacket
- ❏ Sunscreen
- ❏ Contact lens care supplies (It's amazing how many forget!)
- ❏ Water bottles and/or Gatorade
- ❏ Hat and/or sunglasses
- ❏ Other needs as appropriate to your destination

☞ Spending money should be limited to under $50. Stipulate that if there is a theft, each student is fully and totally responsible for his or her own losses.

☞ CD players, video cameras, etc. are also the responsibility of the person bringing them.

Family Donations

☞ Ask parents to donate either chili or spaghetti sauce that is frozen in cardboard half gallon milk or juice containers. We ask for two-thirds of the donations to be with meat and one-third meatless.

☞ Ask each family to donate a bag of fruit and a bakery item (i.e., one or more loaves of bread, a package of hot dog buns, a large bag of bagels, etc.).

☞ Ask parents to loan the tools needed for the week. Mark the tools and take responsibility for their return.

The Prepacking

☞ On the afternoon or evening prior to leaving hold a two-hour packing session. Ask for parent assistance.

☞ Instruct students to pack everything in nylon duffel bags. Regular suitcases are harder to pack. Each student is allowed to bring:
   ❏ One large bag, tagged by student at the prepacking;
   ❏ A sleeping bag packed in a garbage bag, also tagged;
   ❏ A carry-on tote bag or school backpack and a pillow are allowed to be taken on the vehicles the next day.

The prepack should be an orderly process. Students arrive with their parents and check in at each of four stations:
   • Station One: all forms and money collected;
   • Station Two: food donations turned in;
   • Station Three: mark and turn in tools;
   • Station Four: make tags for their personal luggage; take duffel bags and sleeping bags to the trailer to be packed.

Save yourself a lot of grief caused by last-minute mistakes and require the prepack for everyone. If someone cannot make the prepack, require that they arrive early on departure day.

Fun Times

Our trips are famous for some special features and certain SOPs (standard operating practices) that have become a big part of each camp.

☞ Having some "trip products," such as a particular beverage or food or a special restaurant, seems to build a trip identity.

☞ Look for places to visit in the locale or along the way that can give an idea of the flavor of life in the region. Museums, special historic sites, even parks provide an adventure in the new place and are a great way to round out the trip.

Fellowship and Worship

- ☞ Worship with a local congregation on the trip.
- ☞ Bible studies should be a part of most evenings. These are amazing times of community and are important memory watersheds for the students long after the work camp. A number have told me later that the work camp sharing times helped them find God's call and direction for their lives.
- ☞ Provide fellowship time. Make sure evening fun times are shared. Spend time playing games, swimming, preparing meals and cleaning up, or walking as a group.
- ☞ Schedule quiet time for students to reflect on the day's activity or Bible study, to journal their thoughts, to write home, or to simply rest.

The Checklist

This checklist will help you envision and organize your work camp. These are not complete, as every trip is different, but they do examine the major aspects of most trips. Answering these questions will help you plan.

Pretrip Details

1. Destination and type of work?

2. Where will the group stay?
   a. How much will it cost?
   b. Are there boys' and girls' rooms?
   c. Or will the students be sharing a large room?

3. How will the group be transported?
   Rentals needed: Trailers? Vans?

4. Which week will you work? Plan around conflicts with school practices such as band camp, sports training, family vacations, etc.

5. Who will be the adult leaders?
   Who is the contact at the work-camp location?

6. How will meals be provided?
   a. Will the group self-cook?
   b. Will the camp location offer food service?
   c. What is the menu for the week?
   d. Consider special diets for vegetarians, special needs or food allergies.

7. What documents are needed?
   a. Permission slips, birth certificates, health coverage information and generic release forms are all important information and need to be carried with you.
   b. Birth certificates or passports needed if leaving U.S. borders.
   c. Have all documents in hand well before leaving and file them in a transportable file.

8. Who will show and supervise the work sites?
   a. Will there be a person assigned to your group to be a trip guide?
   b. Understand these details fully before leaving home.

9. Organize a phone chain or contacts back home to communicate with the families. Call one designated parent who then gives trip updates, problems or changes to the families.

10. What are the cultural differences?
    a. Is there a language difference?
    b. Is the camp in a different region of the U.S.? Do not offend others by being culturally ignorant even within U.S. culture. There are lots of regional differences between the Midwest, the South, New England, the Pacific Northwest, the West Coast, etc.

Registration and Budget Planning

Budget Items to Consider

1. Transportation

☛ Gasoline expense is figured by the following formula based on the average mileage per gallon of the van, bus or vehicle being driven: Total miles to be traveled, divided by the mileage per gallon (mpg), times the estimated cost for gasoline per gallon.

Example: A trip of 1200 miles in a bus that gets 7 mpg with gasoline at $1.30 per gallon is $1200 \div 7 \times \$1.30 = \$222.85$ estimated to get there and back.

☛ Towing a trailer will reduce mpg.
☛ Gasoline prices are often higher in the summertime.
☛ Figure the expense for each vehicle making the trip for your estimated transportation total.
☛ Plan for tolls, oil and other travel expenses.

2. Food on the road

☛ Budget an amount, say $4 per person per meal for fast food on the road, and tell students if they want more food, they need to pay the extra.
☛ Ask parents to donate a food item and supplement with sandwich fixings. Stop at a park or highway rest stop. Besides saving time and money, it gives students a chance to stretch their legs.
☛ Have students bring a sack lunch for the first lunch out. Provide cold drinks for them.

3. Cost of housing

☛ Churches seem to be the most common sleep accommodations and many will let you stay for free or very inexpensively.

☛ Be good guests: clean up after yourselves, donate time or money to the church, tip the custodian and pay for long distance phone calls that may have been made.

☛ Showers are *essential*. If there are no available showers, either budget to visit a recreation center, school gym or YMCA facility to pay for showers, or arrange to have the campers shower in the homes of church members.

4. Materials and special tools

☛ Some work camp destinations may not have sufficient money to provide materials and tools. Set aside some money to supplement materials and tools if needed.

5. Evening fun, big dinner out/day off

☛ Budget a visit to museums or other local points of interest during the down times.

☛ Ask the contact person or agency what they recommend and try to get them to make the arrangements. They might be able to get discounts.

☛ The group also needs what we call the "Big Night Out!" For the Big Night Out, take the group to a fancy/fun restaurant and give them a $12 allowance for food/fun.

6. Emergency funds

☛ Plan $300 to $500 for emergencies if your church does not have a charge card.

Miscellaneous Details

☛ Enlist leaders who possess some building skills and knowledge. There is nothing worse than getting to a work camp site to find that no one has any idea what to do. It happens way too often.

☛ Schedule the day to include work teams for shopping for groceries, preparing and cleaning up meals and running after materials, as well as working on the actual project.

☛ Treat all job assignments with equal importance and reinforce the teamwork aspect of sharing responsibilities.

☛ Rotate the work teams to allow everyone experience in each aspect of the trip.

☛ Contingency plans are important when work is scheduled for outdoors. A day or two of rain could ruin the most carefully planned experience. So make sure some inside work is possible. Sometimes a rain out can be salvaged by changing the day off.

Work Camp Planning Schedule

Nine to Twelve Months Before

Begin talking about work camp. Teach some studies about missions. Encourage the adult and student leaders to remember the camp in prayer. Ask leaders to start looking into possible work camp locations and gathering information.

Six to Nine Months Before

Continue in prayer. Begin talking about work camp possibilities with your youth group. Have an interest sign-up, telling students that the list is not binding, but that it will be the list from which the work camp is staffed. Send a letter to the parents informing them that work camp is coming. Narrow down the potential work camp list to two places of high interest and a third for standby. Call the three locations and talk directly with the person in charge.

Three to Six Months Before

Gather the campers together for a location selection meeting. Have participants consider each possible location and vote on the one they would like to attend. Assign small groups to plan menus, side trips, equipment needed, materials and donations. Help them to meet regularly. Hold a parents' information meeting to discuss costs, adult advisors, the work, the budget, donations and tools needed, how to pack and details that will satisfy the parents' concerns for the safety of their kids.

Three Months to Three Weeks Before

Continue detailed planning. Check the small groups' progress. Continue to pray for the trip. Keep in contact with the person or agency sponsoring your trip and begin to collect specific details of the work you will do.

Two to Three Weeks Before

Hold a family picnic and cook out. Play a few family games. Use this time as the final meeting before leaving on the work camp to fully inform parents of the details of the trip. Hand out the packing lists, food donations and tool lists. Give them an information

sheet with the descriptions of the vans or bus and their license numbers, the route, the information on the work camp locations and the itinerary. This data is essential if an emergency occurs in which a parent must contact you en route.

Day Before

Hold a two-hour prepack for packing the vans and trailers. Collect fees, birth certificates, medical release forms, insurance information, food donations and other items you have requested. Try to get as much paperwork as possible done beforehand.

Departure Day

Ask the families to be there promptly at the agreed-upon time. Do a last check of fees and forms. Do a head count to make sure everyone is there! We once left with two guys still sleeping at home.

Before pulling out, ask the families to join you in a prayer circle. Thank God for the students, their supportive families and the opportunity to make a difference in the world. Pray for safety and God's leading.

Get Moving!

Day One (usually Saturday)—Likely spent in travel. Check in at your work-camp site and relax.

Day Two (usually Sunday)—Perhaps more travel, then check in. Plan worship time if it is Sunday. Afternoon may be time to visit work sites, do something with a local youth group, or just chill.

Days Three to Five (usually Monday, Tuesday and Wednesday)—Work as directed by the contact person or agency. Evening is time for sharing, study and play.

Day Six (usually Thursday)—Day off to visit an exciting regional place. We most often do our Big Dinner Out on this day. Don't be driven! Relax.

Day Seven (usually Friday)—Finish all scheduled work! Students will adopt the project and feel cheated if they don't get to finish the project.
- Spend the evening cleaning up the sleeping facilities and packing.
- After dinner, have a reflection time and let each one tell what the camp has meant to him or her.
- Close with communion.
- Insist that students sleep—or at least that they let you and the other drivers sleep.

Day Eight (and maybe Day Nine)—Hit the road! Remember to begin discussing next year's work camp while you have momentum.

The Sunday After Work Camp

Have participants share about their adventure in the regular worship services. Thank the church for its prayer and financial support.

Two Weeks After

Hold a family picnic. Have students talk about the trip and share how it changed them. Tell them to get double prints of their pictures and allow them to trade shots. Show videos/slides.

Within a Month

Start planning for next year's life-changing adventure.

Missions and Service Resources

Mission and Service Organizations

Adventure in Missions

6000 Wellspring Trail
Gainesville, GA 30506
(770) 983-1060
Target Work Group: Junior high, high school
Projects: Vacation Bible School, evangelism and construction
Time Span: One to two weeks
Mission Field: U.S. and Latin America

Appalachia Service Project

4523 Bristol Highway
Johnson City, TN 37601
(423) 854-8800
Target Work Group: High school
Projects: Home repair and construction
Time Span: One week
Mission Field: Kentucky, Tennessee, Virginia and West Virginia

AMOR Ministries

1664 Precision Park Lane
San Diego, CA 92173
(619) 662-1200
Target Work Group: High school and college
Projects: Home building
Time Span: One to four days
Mission Field: Mexico

Center for Student Missions

P. O. Box 900
Dana Point, CA 92629
(949) 248-8200
Target Work Group: Junior high, high school and college
Projects: Vacation Bible School, food distribution and children's ministries
Time Span: Customized
Mission Field: Los Angeles; San Francisco; Chicago; Houston; Nashville; Washington, D.C.; and Toronto, Canada

City Team Ministries

Three locations:

2302 Zanker Rd., Suite 206	P. O. Box 627	634 Sproul St.
San Jose, CA 95131-1136	Jonesboro, AR 72406	Chester, PA 19013
(408) 232-5600	(870) 932-4357	(610) 872-6865

Target Work Group: High school and college
Projects: Food and clothing distribution centers, rescue missions, men's and women's rehabilitation programs and homes for unwed mothers
Time Span: Three-month summer internship
Mission Field: Inner cities

Food for the Hungry

7729 E. Greenway Rd.
Scottsdale, AZ 85260
(800) 2-HUNGER (248-6437)
Target Work Group: High school and college
Projects: Construction, Vacation Bible School and spiritual outreach
Time Span: Ten days to two weeks
Mission Field: Worldwide

Hope Mission Outreach

P. O. Box 73
Bethany, MO 64424
(660) 425-2277
Target Work Group: Junior high and high school
Projects: Vacation Bible School, evangelism, medical, construction, sewing and music
Time Span: One week
Mission Field: Worldwide

Inner City Impact

2704 W. North Ave.
Chicago, IL 60647
(773) 384-4200
Target Work Group: All ages
Projects: Backyard clubs, evangelism and construction
Time Span: Customized
Mission Field: Inner-city Chicago

Institute of Outreach Ministries

901 E. Alosta
Azusa, CA 91702
(626) 969-3434
Target Work Group: Junior high, high school and college
Projects: Vacation Bible school, construction and evangelism
Time Span: One week
Mission Field: Mexico

International Teams

411 W. River Rd.
Elgin, IL 60123
(847) 870-3800
Target Work Group: College and career (20-36 years of age) and second careers (over 40 years)
Projects: Church planting, refugee and ethnic minorities, youth work and training, urban/inner city and economic development
Time Span: Summer and two-year programs with career options available
Mission Field: Eastern and Western Europe, Latin America, Central Asia and Southeast Asia

Mountain T.O.P.

2704 Twelfth Ave. South
Nashville, TN 37204
(615) 298-5068
Target Work Group: Junior high, high school and adult
Projects: Construction
Time Span: One week
Mission Field: Tennessee

New Tribes Mission

1000 E. First St.
Sanford, FL 32771
(407) 323-3430
Target Work Group: Fifteen years and up
Projects: Tribal work, construction of homes, schools and airstrips
Time Span: Four to six weeks
Mission Field: Worldwide

Spectrum Ministries

2610 Galveston St.
San Diego, CA 92110
(619) 276-1385
Target Work Group: Junior high, high school and college
Projects: Children's ministry, food distribution, health care, evangelism, rehabilitation centers and jail ministries
Time Span: One-day trips and customized lengths of time
Mission Field: Mexico

Teen Mania Ministries

P. O. Box 2000
Garden Valley, TX 75771
(800) 299-TEEN (299-8336)
Target Work Group: Offers trips to individuals with some available to youth groups
Projects: Evangelism and construction of churches
Time Span: One month
Mission Field: Worldwide

Teen Missions in Canada, Inc.

(A division of Teen Missions International, see below)
P. O. Box 128, Station A
Windsor, ON N9A6KI
(519) 966-7108

Teen Missions International

885 E. Hall Rd.
Merritt Island, FL 32953
(407) 453-0350
Target Work Group: Elementary, junior high, high school and college
Projects: Bible School, drama, construction, evangelism and clown ministries
Time Span: One week to one month
Mission Field: Worldwide

Teen World Outreach (TWO)

P. O. Box 57A
Lima, NY 14485
(716) 582-2792
Target Work Group: Individuals and youth (groups of eight or more can get a group discount)
Projects: Work projects, Vacation Bible School, children's ministries and evangelism
Time Span: Four to seven weeks
Mission Field: Worldwide

Voice of Calvary Ministry

1655 St. Charles St.
Jackson, MS 39209
(601) 353-1635
Target Work Group: High school and adult
Projects: Construction
Time Span: One week
Mission Field: West Jackson, Mississippi

World Vision 30-Hour Famine

P. O. Box 70094
Tacoma, WA 98481-0094
(800) 7-FAMINE (732-6463)
In Canada: (800) 387-8080
www.30hourfamine.org
Target Work Group: Junior high and high school
Projects: Planned famine
Time Span: 30 hours
Mission Field: At your church

Youth With A Mission (YWAM)

12750 W. Sixty-Third Ave.
Arvada, CO 80004
(303) 424-1144

Target Work Group: The listed projects accept high school groups or individuals

Projects: Evangelism and children's ministry or the following sample of projects sponsored by YWAM:

1. **Homes of Hope, Tijuana, Mexico**

   The youth group raises $2,500 and YWAM supplies the materials, tools and staff person to help your team build a home for a needy family in Tijuana. A promotional video is available through: Youth With A Mission; Homes of Hope Program; P. O. Box 8873; Chula Vista, CA 91912; (619) 635-6786.

2. **Discipleship Training Schools**

   These are five- to six-month short-term missions experiences that include a three-month training and teaching phase and a two- to three-month outreach phase. This is available for those who have graduated from high school.

3. **Inner City Ministry**

   YWAM San Francisco customizes inner-city trips for youth groups. Contact Youth With A Mission; 357 Ellis St.; San Francisco, CA 94102; (415) 885-6585.

4. **Gleanings for the Hungry**

   Youth groups can come for a week during the summer to help process dried fruits and vegetables that will be shipped to the hungry around the world. Contact Fruit Dehydration Plant; P. O. Box 309; Sultana, CA 93666; (209) 591-5009.

5. The **"Go Manual"** lists hundreds of mission opportunities with YWAM around the world. Call the YWAM headquarters at (303) 424-1144.

Time Span: Customized
Mission Field: Worldwide

YUGO Ministries

P. O. Box 25
San Dimas, CA 91773
(909) 592-6621

Target Work Group: All ages
Projects: Construction, sports, women's ministries and Vacation Bible School
Time Span: One week
Mission Field: Mexico

Courses, Conferences and Seminars

Worldwide Perspectives—Understanding God's Purposes in the World from Genesis to Exodus

This course is offered in various cities across the United States. It is a 15-week course on understanding your role in worldwide evangelization. It is sponsored by:

The U. S. Center for World Mission
1605 E. Elizabeth St.
Pasadena, CA 91104
(626) 797-1111

Urbana Missions Conference

Offered once every three years the last week of December in Urbana, Illinois. Contact:

InterVarsity Christian Fellowship
P. O. Box 7895
Madison, WI 53707-7895
(608) 274-7995

Short-Term Mission Conference

A training tool for leaders on how to do short-term mission projects. Contact:

VELA Ministries International
P. O. Box 361628
Milpitas, CA 95036-1628
(408) 995-5090
vela@vela.org

Institute of Outreach Ministry (I. O. M.)

I. O. M. hosts missions conferences for senior high youth. Contact:

I. O. M.
Azusa Pacific University
901 E. Alosta Ave.
Azusa, CA 91702
(626) 812-3027

Night of Missions

Your church can sponsor a Night of Missions presented by a Youth With A Mission (YWAM) team. It is a 90-minute program that helps motivate and enhance your emphasis on missions using creative drama, music, testimonies of frontline missionaries and a challenging speaker. Contact:

Night of Missions
11141 Osborne St.
Lake View Terrace, CA 91342
(818) 897-0282

Printed Resources

The following list of printed resources is only a small representation of the many books available on the subject of missions. Please refer to the bibliography in the back of this book for a more complete listing.

PERIODICALS AND NEWSLETTERS

Mission Frontiers

A bimonthly bulletin highlighting news, events, leaders and ideas from the U. S. Center for World Missions and the A.D. 2000 and Beyond movement. Individual subscriptions are $4.00 per year. Contact:
> U. S. Center for World Missions
> 1605 E. Elizabeth St.
> Pasadena, CA 91104
> (818) 797-1111

The Great Commission Handbook

Helpful mission articles as well as an overview chart of various short-term mission opportunities for the coming year. Published every fall.
> Berry Publishing Services
> 701 Main St.
> Evanston, IL 60202
> (708) 869-1573

The Voice of the Martyrs

A monthly newletter containing updated information on the persecuted Church throughout the world.
> The Voice of Martyrs
> P. O. Box 443
> Bartlesville, OK 74005
> (918) 337-8015

RECOMMENDED BOOKS

The following list of resources is only a small representation of the many books available on the subject of missions. Please refer to the bibliography in the back of this book for a more complete listing.

Biographies of Missionaries

The William Carey Library Resource Catalog lists biographies of missionaries, as well as many other resources. Contact:

William Carey Library
P. O. Box 40129
Pasadena, CA 91114
(818) 798-0819
or 1-800-MISSION

Mission Mobilizers Handbook

Published by the William Carey Library, this resource also lists several resources, including other mission periodicals, books, videos, etc. Contact the address/phone number above.

A Mind for Missions

Another book to help stretch a youth worker's worldview, written by Paul Borthwick (Colorado Springs: NavPress Publishing, 1987).

Six Dangerous Questions to Transform Your View of the World

Written by Paul Borthwick (Downers Grove, Ill.: InterVarsity Press, 1997).

Operation World

This resource can be used along with the Joshua Project 2000 to encourage your youth group to adopt an unreached people group, find out all they can about the people group they have chosen and begin to pray as a youth group to adopt an unreached people group. Written by Patrick Johnstone (Grand Rapids, Mich.: Zondervan Publishing House, 1993).

Ideas for Social Action

Written by Tony Campolo and available through Youth Specialties (1224 Greenfield Dr.; El Cajon, CA 92021; 800-255-9884, 1983.)

50 Ways You Can Share Your Faith

Written by Tony Campolo and Gordon Aeschliman (Downers Grove, Ill.: InterVarsity Press, 1993).

50 Ways to Feed a Hungry World

Written by Tony Campolo and Gordon Aeschliman (Downers Grove, Ill.: InterVarsity Press, 1993).

Simulation Games, Dramas and Educational Strategies

CALEB PROJECT RESOURCES

The following three presentations as well as other demonstrations, scripts and dramatizations are available through:

Caleb Project
10 West Dry Creek Circle
Littleton, CO 80120
(303) 730-4170

Worldview Demonstration

This demonstration involves 11 people from the audience and two narrators to show the number of Muslims, Hindus, Buddhists, tribal peoples, Chinese and Christians in the world. It illustrates the imbalance of the distribution of the ministry force today. Lasts approximately 11 minutes.

"Name Above All Names" by Chuck Girard

A mime who shows God's heart for all people groups. Demonstrates how some are called to go, some to pray and some to send. It requires a tape of the song and involves four people and four minutes of your time.

"God's Heart for the Nations"

A choral reading that uses verses from Genesis to Revelation to show it has been God's eternal purpose to redeem people from every nation or people group. Involves four people and four minutes of your time.

DRAMAS AND SKITS

"Yardwork" and "A Missions Carol"

Both scripts show God's heart for the world. Available through:
> Advancing Churches in Mission Commitment (ACMC)
> P. O. Box ACMC
> Wheaton, IL 60189
> (800) 798-2262

"Who Will Fill Your Shoes?"

This is a collection of 13 dramatic sketches for missions awareness. Available through:
> New Hope
> P. O. Box 12065
> Birmingham, AL 35202-2065
> (205) 991-4933

"Gospel Enterprises"

This Star Trek-based skit explains trends in missions. Contact:
> Kevin Guttman
> 11571 College Ave.
> Garden Grove, CA 92640
> (714) 530-1375

CURRICULUM

A Sunday for the World! by Bill Stearns

This is an all-in-one reproducible resource for a missions awareness Sunday involving the whole church. It includes age-appropriate Sunday School lessons (one for each age group from nursery to adult), a leadership session for church leaders, outlines and ideas for the Sunday service, a small-group study guide, a family activity guide, a prayer guide and a list of resources. Published by Gospel Light. To order call 1-800-4-GOSPEL or contact your local Christian bookstore.

Video Resources

"Homeless"

A Power Surge Video
   Media Int.
   313 East Broadway, Suite 207
   Glendale, CA 91209

"EE Taow"

Shows how one tribe responded to the gospel. Features short-term missions and New Tribes Mission (Length: 34 minutes).
   New Tribes Mission
   1000 E. First St.
   Sanford, FL 32771-1487

"The Greatest Story Never Told"

By Gospel Films (Length: 45 minutes)
   Gospel Films
   P. O. Box 455
   Muskegon, MI 48443-0455

"Peace Child"

Also by Gospel Films (Length: 30 minutes)

"Faith Under Fire"

A dramatic portrayal of today's suffering Church throughout the world; includes four true stories of believers suffering for their faith (Length: 30 minutes).
   Voice of the Martyrs
   P. O. Box 443
   Bartlesville, OK 74005

Radical Christianity

A three-part video series for youth by Jim Burns based on his book by the same title (formerly titled *Radically Committed*).
> Gospel Light
> 2300 Knoll Drive
> Ventura, CA 93003
> 800-4-GOSPEL

You Can Make a Difference

A four-part video series by Tony Campolo with a study guide by Denny Rydberg.
> Word Education Products
> (800) 433-3327

"Survival Guide for Teenagers— Our World: The Big Picture"

Priority One International
P. O. Box 796009
Dallas, TX 75379
(214) 423-3800

2100 Productions

"To Every People" introduces four major cultural groups in the world: tribal, Hindu, Muslim and Chinese.

"God So Loved the World" shows God's heart for the urban world (14 minutes).

"God Is Building a City" introduces God's heart for the urban world (14 minutes).

> 2100 Productions (a Division of InterVarsity)
> P. O. Box 7895
> Madison, WI 53707-7895
> (800) 828-2100

Mars Hill Productions

"The Call" shows how God used one girl to influence a generation for Christ.

"Generation" is a series of five videos (10 to 20 minutes each) that chronicle four movements of God among today's generation of young people—a generation called to prayer, to purity, to stand for Christ on their campuses and to take the gospel to every nation.

These two resources are available from:
Mars Hill Productions
12705 South Kirkwood, Suite 218
Stafford, TX 77477

"The Good Seed"

This is the true story of dramatic results through God's working in the Tzetal people of Mexico after the Bible was translated into their language (30 minutes).
Wycliffe Bible Translators
P. O. Box 2727
Huntington Beach, CA 92647-0727
(714) 969-4600

"Doing Your Bit"

This gives a brief overview of people-group thinking and the adopt-a-people strategy. It is entertaining and clearly educational for youth and adults (10 minutes). Produced by True Colours Productions; distributed by:
U. S. Center for World Missions
1605 E. Elizabeth St.
Pasadena, CA 91104
800-MISSION

Other Videos

Check the U. S. Center for World Missions and InterVarsity 2100 Productions listings in the William Carey Library Resource Catalog.

The Acts 1:8 Model for Missions

One way to make sure you have a balanced missions and service program is to use the model found in Acts 1:8: "You will receive power when the Holy Spirit comes on you; and you will be my witnesses in Jerusalem, and in all Judea and Samaria, and to the ends of the earth."

Although there may be several ways to organize this balance, here is an example of how this could work:

In Jerusalem: The Local Congregation

Suggested mission or service projects:

Mission to the Elderly

Church Nursery Makeover

Baby-sitting Service

Big Brother/Big Sister

Adopt a Sick Person

In All Judea: The Local Community

Suggested mission or service projects:

Toy Collection

Community Vacation Bible School

Hospital Visitation

Adopt a Park

Food/Clothing Bank

School Campus

In Samaria: A Different Culture

Suggested mission or service projects:

Inner-city Outreach

Migrant Worker Camps

Soup Kitchen

Exceptional Children/Adult Homes
Native American Reservations

To the Ends of the Earth: International Opportunities

Suggested mission or service projects:

Sponsor a Child

Mexico Outreach

Building a House in Mexico

Adopt an Unreached People Group

Mission Trip to Another Country

Bible References for Studies on Missions and Service

Power Through Praise and Worship—2 Chronicles 20:1-26; Psalm 149:6

God's Heart for the City—Jeremiah 29:4-7; Isaiah 65:17-22

Compassion/Sending Out Workers—Matthew 9:35-38

The Least of These—Matthew 25:31-46

Equipped to Go!—Matthew 28:18-20; John 20:19-31; Acts 1:8

Why Do We Serve Jesus?—Luke 7:36-50

Parable of the Good Samaritan—Luke 10:25-37

What's More Important than Serving?—Luke 10:38-42

Relating and Communicating the Gospel—John 4:1-42

Taking Up the Towel—John 13:1-7,12-17

Service and Humility—Philippians 2:1-11

Favoritism: Winners and Losers—James 2:1-13

Faith and Deeds—James 2:14-26

Inductive Study on the Books of James and 1 John

Bibliographies

Note: The following list of printed resources is from a list provided by Urbana Missions Conferences.[1] It was published in 1993 so some of the publications listed may no longer be in print. Those resources have been designated with an asterisk (*). Books that are out of print may still be available from libraries, bookstores or the publishers. William Carey Library in Pasadena, California (1-800-MISSION) is also a source of books on missions and missionaries.

Periodicals

Evangelical Missions Information Service (EMIS), Box 794, Wheaton, IL 60187 publishes the following:
- *Evangelical Missions Quarterly*, a missions-oriented magazine
- *Missionary News Service*, a semimonthly missionary news source
- *Pulse*, a semimonthly world news service

Global Prayer Digest, Frontier Fellowship, 1605 Elizabeth St., Pasadena, CA 91104. A daily devotional and prayer guide featuring unreached people groups.

Great Commission Handbook, Berry Publishing, 701 Main St., Evanston, IL 60202. An annual of informative articles about short-term missions; includes listings of service opportunities.

Prism, 10 Lancaster Ave., Wynwood, PA 19096. A monthly (10 issues per year) magazine challenging Christians to live out the gospel in a contemporary society.

World Christian Magazine, P. O. Box 3278, Ventura, CA 93006.

Note: Many missions agencies and denominations publish magazines. Ask them to put you on their mailing list.

Books

General Reading

Bryant, David. *Stand in the Gap*. Ventura, CA: Regal Books, 1997.

*Campolo, Tony and Gordon Aeschliman. *101 Ways Your Church Can Change the World*. Ventura, CA: Regal Books, 1993.

———. *50 Ways to Share Your Faith*. Downers Grove, IL: InterVarsity Press, 1993.

*———. *50 Ways You Can Feed a Hungry World*. Downers Grove, IL: InterVarsity Press, 1991.

———. *50 Ways You Can Reach Your World*. Downers Grove, IL: InterVarsity Press, 1993.

*Cooper, Anne. *Ishmael My Brother: A Biblical Course on Islam*. Monrovia, CA: MARC (A Division of World Vision International), 1985.

Duewel, Wesley. *Touch the World Through Prayer*. Grand Rapids, MI: Zondervan Publishing House, 1986.

Eaton, Chris and Hurst, Kim. *Vacations With a Purpose*. Colorado Springs: NavPress Publishing Group, 1991.

Fernando, Ajith. *Spiritual Living in a Secular World*. Grand Rapids, MI: Zondervan Publishing House, 1993.

Griffiths, Michael. *Tinker, Tailor, Missionary: Options in a Changing World*. InterVarsity Press, United Kingdom, 1993.

Hancock, Robert L., ed. *The Ministry of Development in Evangelical Perspective on the Social and Spiritual Mandate*. Pasadena, CA: William Carey Library, 1979.

*Harrison, Dan. *Strongest in the Broken Places*. Downers Grove, IL: InterVarsity Press, 1989.

Heselgrave, David. *Communicating Christ Cross-Culturally*. Grand Rapids, MI: Zondervan Publishing House, 1991.

Hiebert, Paul G. *Anthropological Insights for Missionaries*. Grand Rapids, MI: Baker Book House, 1985.

Johnstone, Patrick. *Operation World*. Grand Rapids, MI: Zondervan Publishing House, 1993.

Jordan, Peter. *Re-Entry*. Seattle, WA: YWAM Publishing (A Division of Youth With A Mission International), 1992.

*Kane, J. Herbert. *Wanted: World Christians*. Grand Rapids, MI: Baker Book House, 1986.

*Kershaw, Max. *How to Share the Good News With Your Muslim Friend*. Colorado Springs: International Students Inc., 1990.

*Lau, Lawson. *The World at Your Doorstep*. Downers Grove, IL: InterVarsity Press, 1989.

Lingenfelter, Sherwood G. and Marvin K. Mayers. *Ministering Cross-Culturally: An Incarnational Model for Personal Relationships*. Grand Rapids, MI: Baker Book House, 1986.

*MacLeod, Meri. *Becoming Friends With an International Student*. Colorado Springs: International Students Inc., 1990.

Mayers, Marvin K. *Christianity Confronts Culture*. Grand Rapids, MI: Zondervan Publishing House, 1974.

McNeill, Don, Morrison, Douglas A. and Nouwen, Henri J. *Compassion: A Reflection on the Christian Life*. New York City: Doubleday & Co., Inc., 1982.

McQuilken, Robertson. *The Great Omission*. Grand Rapids, MI: Baker Book House, 1984.

*Newbingen, Lesslie. *Foolishness to the Greeks: The Gospel and Western Culture*. Grand Rapids, MI: William B. Eerdmans Publishing Co., 1986.

*Parshall, Phil. *New Paths in Muslim Evangelism*. Grand Rapids, MI: Baker Book House, 1980.

Perkins, Spencer and Rice, Chris. *More Than Equals: Racial Healing for the Sake of the Gospel*. Downers Grove, IL: InterVarsity Press, 1993.

*Pirolo, Neil. *Serving the Senders*. San Diego, CA: Emmaus Road, International, 1991.

*Saunders, Ray. *Lord of the Abandoned*. Ada, MI: Chosen Books (A Division of Baker Book House), 1991.

Sheikh, Bilquis. *I Dared Call Him Father*. Ada, MI: Chosen Books (A Division of Baker Book House), 1978.

Sider, Ronald J. *Rich Christians in an Age of Hunger: A Biblical Study*, third edition. Dallas, TX: Word Publishing (A Division of Thomas Nelson, Inc.), 1990.

Sider, Ronald J. *One-Sided Christianity?: Uniting the Church to Heal a Lost and Broken World*. Grand Rapids, MI: Zondervan Publishing House, 1993.

*Stafford, Tim. *The Friendship Gap*. Downers Grove, IL: InterVarsity Press, 1984.

Stepping Out: A Guide to Short-Term Missions. Seattle, WA: YWAM Publishing (A Division of Youth With A Mission International), 1992.

The Short-Term Mission Handbook. Evanston, IL: Berry Publishing Services, 1992.

Winter, Ralph D. and Steve Hawthorne, ed. *Perspectives on the World Christian Movement*. Pasadena, CA: William Carey Library, 1994.

Wolterstorff, Nicholas. *Until Justice and Peace Embrace*. Grand Rapids, MI: William B. Eerdmans Publishing Co., 1983.

Yamamori, Tetsunao. *God's New Envoys*. Downers Grove, IL: InterVarsity Press, 1993.

Zacharias, Ravi. *A Shattered Visage: The Real Face of Atheism*. Grand Rapids, MI: Baker Book House, 1993.

Missionary Biographies

*Armitage, Carolyn. *Straight for the Goal: The Life Story of David Adeney*. Wheaton, IL: Harold Shaw Publications, 1993.

*Hoadley-Dick, Lois, and Carmichael, Amy. *Let the Little Children Come*. Chicago: Moody Press, 1984.

*Lewis, Karen, and Hathersmith, June. *Harvest of Trust*. Huntington Beach, CA: Wycliffe Bible Translators, 1987.

*Magnuson, Sally. *The Flying Scotsman: A Biography of Eric Lidell*. United Kingdom: Quartet Books, Inc., 1982.

Miller, Basil. *William Carey*. Minneapolis, MN: Bethany House Publications, 1985.

Miller, Susan M. *Hudson Taylor*. Uhrichsville, OH: Barbour and Co., Inc., 1993.

Olson, Bruce. *Bruchko*. Lake Mary, FL: Creation House, 1973.

Richardson, Don. *Peace Child*. Ventura, CA: Regal Books, 1975.

Richardson, Don. *Eternity in Their Hearts*. Ventura CA: Regal Books, 1984.

*Taylor, Mrs. Howard. *Borden of Yale '09*. Minneapolis, MN: Bethany House Publications, 1988.

*Taylor, Howard, and Taylor, Mary G. *Hudson Taylor's Spiritual Secret*. Chicago: Moody Press.

*Tucker, Ruth. *Guardians of the Great Commission*. Grand Rapids, MI: Zondervan Publishing House, 1983.

Tucker, Ruth. *From Jerusalem to Irian Jaya*. Grand Rapids, MI: Zondervan Publishing House, 1983.

Notes:

1. Taken from *'93 Urbana: Taking It Home Missions Resource Handbook.* Used by permission of Urbana and InterVarsity/U.S.A.

* Denotes that this book may be out of print, but you may still be able to find a copy in libraries, bookstores or from the publishers. The William Carey Library may also be a source of books on missions and missionaries (1-800-MISSION).

Annotated Bibliography

Organizations

Advancing Churches in Missions Commitment; P. O. Box 3929; Peachtree City, GA 30269-7929. Helps churches develop their mission resources and involvement. Their *Church Missions Policy Handbook* offers excellent ideas on missions education for youth.

Bread for the World; 207 E. 16th St.; New York, NY 10003. A Christian agency that lobbies in Congress on behalf of bills that benefit the hungry. Educational materials for high-school groups available.

Center for Student Missions; 27302 Calle Arroyo; San Juan Capistrano, CA 92675. Provides suburban and rural youth, adult and family groups, inner-city missions and service opportunities in some of North America's key urban centers. CSM currently operates full-time ministry centers in Chicago, Houston, Los Angeles, Nashville, San Francisco, Toronto and Washington, D. C.

Compassion International; P. O. Box 7000; Colorado Springs, CO 80933. A relief organization dedicated especially to the care of children. Their Compassion Project assists youth groups in promoting student involvement.

Evangelical Missions Information Service; P. O. Box 794; Wheaton, IL 60189. Their monthly *Pulse* is a vast resource of missionary facts from around the world.

Food for the Hungry; P. O. Box E; Scottsdale, AZ 85252. A hunger-relief organization with innovative programs for young people to serve in.

Institute for Outreach Ministries; Azusa Pacific University; 901 E. Alosta Ave.; Azusa, CA 91702-7000. An outreach organization dedicated to involving young people in missions with an emphasis on reaching the people of Mexico.

Inter-Christo; 19303 Fremont Ave. N.; Seattle, WA 98133. A Christian placement organization that matches skills with positions worldwide.

International Teams; 515 Schoenbeck Road; Prospect Heights, IL 60070-0203. A mission organization with an emphasis on youth ministry, serving the National Institute of Youth Ministry, Reach Out Solutions and Sonlife as a sending agency.

InterVarsity Christian Fellowship; Box 7895; Madison, WI 53707. Producer of videos, especially the addresses of Urbana missions conferences (InterVarsity hosts the Urbana conferences every three years) and the "To Every People" series.

National Institute of Youth Ministry; 32236 Paseo Adelanto, Suite D; San Juan Capistrano, CA 92675. NIYM provides youth worker training, youth events and outreach, parent forums, community support and resources worldwide.

Operation Mobilization; P. O. Box 2277; Peachtree City, GA 30269. One of the largest organizations in the world for involving young people in world missions everywhere.

Quito Center of Youth Ministry; Casilla 17-17-691; Quito, Ecuador; South America. Provides youth worker training, youth events and outreach, parent forums, community support, resources and research both in Spanish and English to communities throughout Latin America.

Reach Out Solutions; 3961 Holcomb Bridge Road, Suite 201; Norcross, GA 30092. A youth ministry training organization based in Atlanta, with excellent training around the world.

Sonlife; 526 N. Main; Elburn, IL 60119. A youth ministry strategy training organization with over a hundred missionaries.

Teen Missions in Canada, Inc.; P. O. Box 128, Station A; Windsor, ON N9A6KI. Canadian division of Teen Missions International (see the following listing).

Teen Missions International; 885 East Hall Road; Merritt Island, FL 32953-8443. The champion of youth-service teams, TMI sends out thousands of young people each summer in teams of 25 to 35 on six- to ten-week projects, virtually everywhere in the world.

U. S. Center for World Missions; 1605 E. Elizabeth St.; Pasadena, CA 91104. A world-renowned resource center on missionary research that offers several publications through the William Carey Library.

World Relief Corporation; Box WRC; Wheaton, IL 60189. The relief arm of the National Association of Evangelicals, WRC offers church groups ways to respond to needy churches around the world.

World Servants; 160 Harbor Dr.; Key Biscayne, FL 33149. Similar to Teen Missions International, but with more of a youth-group-building orientation. Offers shorter terms (two to four weeks) and encourages teams to come from the same youth group or church.

World Vision; P. O. Box 78481; Tacoma, WA 98481-8481. A relief and development organization that has some great programs for youth group fund-raisers, including the "Love Loaf" program and the "30-Hour Famine."

Periodical

Great Commission Handbook. SMS Publications; 701 Main St.; Evanston, IL 60202. An annual of informative articles about short-term missions; includes listings of service opportunities.

Books

Borthwick, Paul. *How to Plan, Develop and Lead a Youth Missionary Team.* Grace Chapel; 3 Militia Drive; Lexington, MA 02420: Grace Chapel, 1981. A short booklet for youth workers that answers key questions about planning their own mission teams.

———. *A Mind for Missions.* Colorado Springs, CO: NavPress, 1987. Easy-to-read blueprint for building world vision. Offers 10 building blocks to use in youth Bible studies or Sunday School.

*———. *Youth and Missions: Expanding Your Students' World View.* Wheaton, IL: Scripture Press, 1988. Explains how to motivate young people toward world missions. (Out of print in the United States.)

Bryant, David. *Stand in the Gap.* Ventura, CA: Regal Books, 1997 (revision of *In the Gap*). Proposes that God wants every Christian to be a world Christian.

———. *Concerts of Prayer.* Ventura, CA: Regal Books, 1988. This book is useful in encouraging prayer for missions.

Crossman, Meg (ed.). *Worldwide Perspectives.* Pasadena, CA: William Carey Library Publishers, 1996. An encyclopedic volume on missions history, theology and current issues. A valuable reference volume on missions.

*Hinchey, Margaret. *Fund Raisers That Work.* Loveland, CO: Group Publishing Inc., 1988. A myriad of ideas on raising money through youth-group activities.

Johnstone, Patrick. *Operation World.* Grand Rapids, MI: Zondervan, 1993. A day-to-day prayer guide that takes you around the world in 365 days.

*Kane, J. Herbert. *Wanted: World Christians!* Grand Rapids, MI: Baker Books, 1986. A guide to building your own vision for and involvement in the world.

Olson, Bruce. *Bruchko.* Carol Stream, IL: Creation House, 1978. Fascinating, inspiring autobiography of a teenager who obeyed God's call to the mission field.

Richardson, Don. *Lords of the Earth.* Ventura, CA: Regal Books, 1985. Stirring missions biography that has enough action to hold a teenager's attention.

———. *Peace Child.* Ventura, CA: Regal Books, 1976. Gripping real-life account of Richardson's adventures sharing the true Peace Child, Christ, with cannibals; very effective with young people.

Stepping Out: A Guide to Short-Term Missions. Monrovia, CA: Short-Term Advocates, 1987. A compendium of various issues related to short-term missions. Most useful for collegians and older.

Tucker, Ruth A. *From Jerusalem to Irian Jaya.* Grand Rapids, MI: Zondervan, 1983. A biographical history of Christian missions. Contains an index of illustrations that is useful when preparing messages.

Notes:
2. Selected bibliography compiled by Paul Borthwick (updated by him, 1998) originally published in the fall 1989 issue of *YouthWorker Journal* © 1989 by CCM Communications. Reprinted with permission. For supplemental information call 800-769-7624.

* Denotes that this book may be out of print, but you may still be able to find a copy in libraries, bookstores or from the publishers. The William Carey Library may also be a source of books on missions and missionaries (1-800-MISSION).

Add a New Member to Your Youth Staff.

Jim Burns is president of the National Institute of Youth Ministry.

Meet Jim Burns. He won't play guitar and he doesn't do windows, but he will take care of your programming needs. That's because his new curriculum, **YouthBuilders Group Bible Studies**, is a comprehensive program designed to take your group through their high school years. (If you have junior high kids in your group, **YouthBuilders** works for them too.)

For less than $6 a month, you'll get Jim Burns' special recipe of high-involvement, discussion-oriented, Bible-centered studies. It's the next generation of Bible curriculum for youth—and with Jim on your staff, you'll be free to spend more time one-on-one with the kids in your group.

Here are some of Youth-Builders' hottest features:

- Reproducible pages—one book fits your whole group
- Wide appeal—big groups, small groups—even adjusts to combine junior high/high school groups
- Hits home—special section to involve parents with every session of the study
- Interactive Bible discovery—geared to help young people find answers themselves
- Cheat sheets—a Bible *Tuck-In*™ with all the session information on a single page
- Flexible format—perfect for Sunday mornings, midweek youth meetings, or camps and retreats
- Three studies in one—each study has three four-session modules that examine critical life choices.

 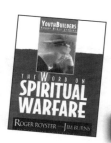 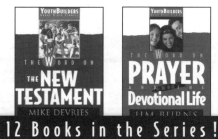  

12 Books in the Series!

The Word on Sex, Drugs & Rock 'N' Roll
ISBN 08307.16424 $16.99

The Word on Prayer and the Devotional Life
ISBN 08307.16432 $16.99

The Word on the Basics of Christianity
ISBN 08307.16440 $16.99

The Word on Being a Leader, Serving Others & Sharing Your Faith
ISBN 08307.16459 $16.99

The Word on Helping Friends in Crisis
ISBN 08307.16467 $16.99

The Word on the Life of Jesus
ISBN 08307.16475 $16.99

The Word on Finding and Using Your Spiritual Gifts
ISBN 08307.17897 $16.99

The Word on the Sermon on the Mount
ISBN 08307.17234 $16.99

The Word on Spiritual Warfare
ISBN 08307.17242 $16.99

The Word on the New Testament
ISBN 08307.17250 $16.99

The Word on the Old Testament
ISBN 08307.17269 $16.99

The Word on Family
ISBN 08307.17277 $16.99

More Great Resources from Jim Burns

Drugproof Your Kids
Stephen Arterburn and Jim Burns

Solid biblical principles are combined with the most effective prevention and intervention techniques to give parents a guide they can trust.
ISBN 08307.17714 $10.99

Drugproof Your Kids Video
A 90-minute seminar featuring Stephen Arterburn and Jim Burns. Includes a reproducible syllabus.
SPCN 85116.00876 $19.99

Parenting Teens Positively
Video *Featuring Jim Burns*

Understand the forces shaping the world of a teenager and what you can do to be a positive influence. This powerful message of hope is for anyone working with—or living with—youth. Includes reproducible syllabus. UPC 607135.000655 $29.99

Surviving Adolescence
Jim Burns

Jim Burns helps teens—and their parents—negotiate the path from adolescence to adulthood with real-life stories that show how to make it through the teen years in one piece. ISBN 08307.20650 $9.99

For these and more great resources and to learn about NIYM's leadership training, call **1-800-397-9725**.

Gospel Light

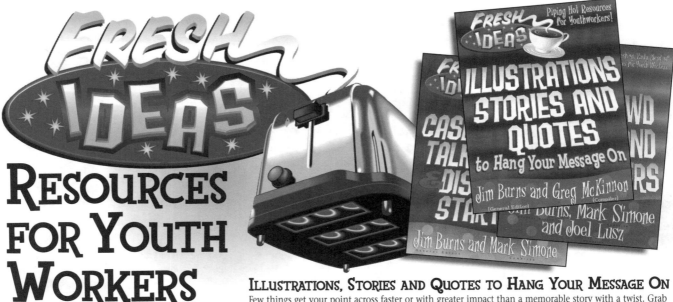

FRESH IDEAS

RESOURCES FOR YOUTH WORKERS

Jim Burns, General Editor

Turn your youth group meetings into dynamic, exciting events that kids look forward to attending week after week! Supercharge your messages, grab their attention with your activities and connect with kids the first time and every time with these great resources. Just try to keep these books on the shelf!

ILLUSTRATIONS, STORIES AND QUOTES TO HANG YOUR MESSAGE ON

Few things get your point across faster or with greater impact than a memorable story with a twist. Grab your teens' attention by talking with your mouth full of unforgettable stories.
Manual, ISBN 08307.18834 **$16.99**

CASE STUDIES, TALK SHEETS AND DISCUSSION STARTERS

Teens learn best when they talk—not when you talk at them. A discussion allowing youth to discover the truth for themselves, with your guidance, is a powerful experience that will stay with them for a lifetime.
Manual, ISBN 08307.18842 **$16.99**

GAMES, CROWDBREAKERS AND COMMUNITY BUILDERS

Dozens of innovative, youth-group-tested ideas for fun and original crowdbreakers, as well as successful plans and trips for building a sense of community in your group.
Manual, ISBN 08307.18818 **$16.99**

More Resources for Youth Workers, Parents & Students

Steering Them Straight
Stephen Arterburn & Jim Burns

Parents can find understanding as well as practical tools to deal with crisis situations. Includes guidelines that will help any family prevent problems before they develop.
UPC 156179.4066 **$10.99**

The Youth Builder
Jim Burns

This Gold Medallion Award winner provides you with proven methods, specific recommendations and hands-on examples of handling and understanding the problems and challenges of youth ministry.
ISBN 089081.1576. **$16.95**

Spirit Wings
Jim Burns

In the language of today's teens, these 84 short devotionals will encourage youth to build a stronger and more intimate relationship with God.
ISBN 08928.37837 **$10.95**

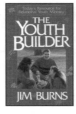

Radical Love
Book & Video, Jim Burns

In *Radical Love* kids discover why it's best to wait on God's timing, how to say no when their bodies say yes and how to find forgiveness for past mistakes.
Paperback, ISBN 08307.17935 **$9.99**
VHS Video, SPCN 85116.00922 **$19.99**

90 Days Through the New Testament
Jim Burns

A growth experience through the New Testament that lays the foundation for developing a daily time with God.
ISBN 08307.14561 **$9.99**

Getting in Touch with God
Jim Burns

Develop a consistent and disciplined time with God in the midst of hectic schedules as Jim Burns shares with you inspiring devotional readings to deepen your love of God.
ISBN 08908.15208 **$2.95**

Radical Christianity
Book & Video, Jim Burns

Radical Christianity is a proven plan to help youth live a life that's worth living and make a difference in their world.
Paperback, ISBN 08307.17927 **$9.99**
VHS Video, SPCN 85116.01082 **$19.99**

The Youth Worker's Book of Case Studies
Jim Burns

Fifty-two true stories with discussion questions to add interest to Bible studies.
ISBN 08307.15827 **$12.99**

To order NIYM resources, please call

1-800-397-9725

or to learn how you can take advantage of NIYM training opportunities call or write to:
NIYM • PO Box 4374 • San Clemente CA
92674 • 714/498-4418

What in the world is *NIYM*?

A.) The Neurotically Inclined Yo-Yo Masters
B.) The Neatest Incidental Yearbook Mystery
C.) The Natural Ignition Yields of Marshmallows
D.) The National Institute of Youth Ministry

If you deliberately picked A, B, or C you're the reason Jim Burns started NIYM! If you picked D, you can go to the next page. In any case, you could learn more about NIYM. Here are some IQ score-raisers:

Jim Burns started NIYM to:
• Meet the growing needs of training and equipping youth workers and parents
• Develop excellent resources and events for young people—in the U.S. and internationally
• Empower young people and their families to make wise decisions and experience a vital Christian lifestyle.

NIYM can make a difference in your life and enhance your youth work skills through these special events:

Institutes—These consist of week-long, in-depth small-group training sessions for youth workers.

Trainer of Trainees—NIYM will train you to train others. You can use this training with your volunteers, parents and denominational events. You can go through the certification process and become an official NIYM associate. (No, you don't get a badge or decoder ring).

International Training—Join NIYM associates to bring youth ministry to kids and adults around the world. (You'll learn meanings to universal words like "yo!" and "hey!')

Custom Training—These are special training events for denominational groups, churches, networks, colleges and seminaries.

Parent Forums—We'll come to your church or community with two incredible hours of learning, interaction and fellowship. It'll be fun finding out who makes your kids tick!

Youth Events—Dynamic speakers, interaction and drama bring a powerful message to kids through a fun and fast-paced day. Our youth events include: This Side Up, Radical Respect, Surviving Adolescence and Peer Leadership.

For brain food or a free information packet about the National Institute of Youth Ministry, write to:

NIYM
P.O. Box 4374 • San Clemente, CA 92674
Tel: (714) 498-4418 • Fax: (714) 498-0037 • NIYMin@aol.com

Why I Sponsor A Child
Through Compassion

As a youth worker, I'm always looking for practical ways to challenge the kids and families I get to be around. Recently, the WWJD (What Would Jesus Do?) Campaign has been immensely popular—almost trendy. Rather than trying to speculate, "what would Jesus do," maybe we should simply respond to the question "what DID He do?" No question but that one of His highest priorities was that of responding to the needs of the "least of these." And, He's challenged us to do the same.

I can't think of anything more important in life than helping impact the world in which we live by meeting the needs of hurting children. Many child sponsorship organizations exist to help people do just that!

Compassion International does it best!

I've had the privilege of visiting some of Compassion's projects in Ecuador. I came away impressed that each project is run exclusively by Christians who are committed to helping each child get the best possible start in life—and an opportunity to receive new life in Jesus Christ.

Just 80 cents a day ($24 a month) provides desperately needy kids access to educational opportunities, health screening, and supplemental food. Great return for a minimal investment. *Smart Money*, a magazine of the *Wall Street Journal*, included Compassion (the only child sponsorship organization) in a list of ten charities they said give the "most bang for your buck!"

But, it's not just about money and good stewardship. This is what I really like about Compassion. Sponsors get to be personally involved by building a relationship with their sponsored child. As a sponsor, you'll receive your child's photo and personal story. You can exchange letters and even send an additional amount for gifts on birthdays or at Christmas. Our entire family looks forward to receiving letters from our sponsored children, Ramiro Moises Santi and Ruth Irlanda Cando Cuenca, and hopes to actually visit them someday. The child you sponsor will know you by name and appreciate your love, help, and prayers.

Won't you join with me in giving a needy child a new start today by completing this coupon or by calling Compassion's toll-free number?

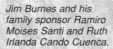

Jim Burnes and his family sponsor Ramiro Moises Santi and Ruth Irlanda Cando Cuenca.

Yes! I want to give a life-changing gift to one child in need.

Please select a child who needs my love and prayers. Send me his or her photo, personal story, and a complete sponsorship packet. If I decide to become a sponsor, I'll send my first monthly sponsorship check for $24 at that time.

My preference is: ❑ a boy ❑ a girl ❑ either
From: ❑ Africa ❑ Asia ❑ South America
❑ Central America ❑ any location

❑ I want to begin immediately.

My first sponsorship support is enclosed as follows: ❑ $24 (one month) ❑ $72 (three months)

Name _____

Address _____

City _____

State _____ Zip _____

Telephone (____) _____

Sponsorship is tax-deductible and receipts will be sent.

QUESTIONS? CALL (800) 336-7676
or visit our Web site at www.compassion.com

COMPASSION™
INTERNATIONAL
Colorado Springs, Colorado 80997

ECFA
CHARTER MEMBER

335975004